LANGUAGE
ON THE
JOB

LANGUAGE ON THE JOB

Balancing Business Needs and Employee Rights

Bill Piatt

University of New Mexico Press
Albuquerque

Library of Congress Cataloging–in–Publication Data

Piatt, Bill.
   Language on the Job: balancing business needs and employee
rights / Bill Piatt.
          p. cm.
   Include index.
   ISBN 08263-1410-4
   1. Discriminationin employment—Law and legislation—United States. 2.
Linguistic minorities—Legal status, laws, etc.—United States.   3.   United
States—language—Law and legislation.
I. TItle.
KF3466.P5   1993
344.73'01133—dc20
[347.3041133   92-28784
                                                                     CIP

Otra vez, para Rosanne, Seana, Bob y Alicia

CONTENTS

Preface

According to the *Wall Street Journal* (November 7, 1989, p. B1) language is rapidly becoming a "sticky issue" in the workplace. Given the ongoing language rights debate in this country, this should come as no surprise. As jobs become more complex, and immigrants and other people with limited English proficiency make up a rising share of the work force, employers, employees and unions will be required to struggle with some basic questions:

(1) Should employers hire people with limited English skills or "foreign" accents?

(2) What happens when employees decide to use their native tongues among themselves, especially in front of co-workers, supervisors or customers?

(3) Must an employer pay a worker an additional increment for the use of the employee's language skill when the employee is required to use that language with customers?

(4) How can a union provide the necessary "duty of fair representation" to employees with limited English skills?

(5) How can all parties equitably resolve the inevitable disputes that will arise as a result of these concerns?

This book is an attempt to analyze these issues and provide useful approaches to their resolution. I bring to this process the spirit and assumptions of my previous law and language writings. That is, I assume that much of the confusion in our present system exists because well-intentioned people do not understand the complex historical, legal, political, philosophical, and economic interests at stake. The resulting confusion creates an unhealthy environment which breeds mistrust and division. Unfortunately, it also provides not so-well-intentioned folks with an opportunity to exploit the confusion and overreact with simplistic and counter-productive measures such as the attempt to impose blanket restrictions against the use of languages other than English.

Another assumption I make from the outset is that demographics and consumer demands will continue to reflect a growing multilingualism in the marketplace. As industry and government seek to meet the increasing demands for multilingual personnel and for marketing and training material, language rights issues will need to be resolved prospectively; the costs and disruptions of litigation make it simply too inefficient. Most of the potential controversies can be anticipated and resolved by agreement in advance. Mechanisms for the equitable resolution of those disputes which cannot be anticipated can be built into such agreements. Where no such agreements exist, parties can make use of options other than litigation for resolving language rights disputes. And, in the unfortunate circumstances where litigation becomes the only method for resolution of the controversies, a knowledge of the legal framework should speed the process.

Perhaps somewhat immodestly I am convinced that a careful examination of the material to come in this book will enable the reader to acquire sufficient understanding of the issues so that potential language rights controversies on the job can be anticipated and fairly resolved.

As we approach these issues, the words of H.G. Wells published in 1920 offer an important perspective:

> There are unhopeful prophets who see in the gathering together of men into one community the possibility of violent race conflicts, — conflicts for ascendancy, but that is to suppose that civilization is incapable of adjustments by which men of different qualities and temperaments and appearances will live side by side, following different roles and contributing diverse gifts. The weaving of mankind into one community does not imply the creation of a homogeneous community, but rather the reverse: the welcome and the adequate utilization of distinctive quality in an atmosphere of under-

standing. It is the almost universal bad manners of the present age which make race intolerable of race. The community to which we may be moving will be more mixed— which does not necessarily mean more interbred — more serious and more interesting than any existing community. Communities all to one pattern, like boxes of toy soldiers, are things of the past rather than the future. — *The Outline of History,* Vol. II, pp. 592–593.

Bill Piatt
January 21, 1992

Acknowledgments

The author gratefully acknowledges the encouragement and assistance of Professor David L. Gregory, St. John's University Law School, and Professor Merrick T. Rossein, City University of New York Law School at Queens College. Texas Tech University School Of Law students who assisted in checking citations include: Carole Cross, Humberto Enriquez, Maria Leyva, Rosemary Marin, Lara Nehman, and Lawrence Piccagli.

Part One

MARKET
PERSPECTIVES

CHAPTER ONE

CHANGING WORKFORCE AND MARKETS

Once again, the American work force is changing, reflecting demographic and economic changes in the American population. Many white males are leaving the work force through retirement, and more women and minorities are entering. Of the twenty million workers who are projected to enter our work force between 1985 and the year 2000, 83 percent will be women, minorities, or immigrants, and only 17 percent will be Caucasian male citizens (Hudson Institute Study). In 1985, 7 percent of all new workers were immigrants; the 1988 Hudson study indicates that 22 percent of those entering the work force between 1985 and the year 2000 will be immigrants. The implications of this greater diversity and particularly the language barriers that employers and employees will have to overcome have begun to surface in litigation, academic studies, and recent articles in the *Wall Street Journal*, the *New York Times*, the *Los Angeles Times*, the *Washington Post*, and many other publications (see the bibliographies following this and other chapters).

Yet in many regards this is a "back to the future" discussion. After all, as a nation of immigrants we have repeatedly and successfully dealt with most of the current concerns about communication and the broader concerns about maintaining national unity notwithstanding the presence of many "foreigners" among us—foreigners who, in fact, eventually become us. What may be different about the present situation (other than, of course, that it is happening to us and not our ancestors), is that communications have become virtually instantaneous. Also, the foreign language population with the highest visibility, Spanish, seems more likely to maintain the use of its language than have other immigrant groups. There is also perhaps a better orchestrated and financed nativist movement around this time seeking to implement a radical departure from this country's tradition of official linguistic neutrality. (The reader is referred to this author's 1990 book *¿ Only English? Law and Language Policy in the United States* for a broader examination of the concerns in the current language rights debate).

In any event, the logical first step in approaching issues related to language-on-the-job is to consider how we have dealt with them in the past. With this perspective we may gain some insight into how employers, employees, unions, courts, and legislatures can reapply what has worked, modify what has not, and avoid repeating past injustices.

Who Are We?

Perhaps the easiest way to identify who we are as a nation and a work force is to clarify who we are not. We are not now, nor have we ever been a monolithic, unilingual, and unicultural nation. Our growth as a nation has occurred as the result of waves of immigrating peoples from many cultural and linguistic backgrounds. Most of this immigration has been voluntary. The exceptions include the reprehensible history of slavery and the annexation of contiguous territories and the people who inhabit them. This process has resulted in the addition of many different peoples throughout our history. The notion that we might wish to accommodate new arrivals to survive and prosper as a nation, then, is not new. In fact, it appears there were more immigrants to this country, in the early years of this century, both in absolute terms and also as a percentage of the overall population, than now. In 1908, for example, more than twice as many people legally immigrated (1.3 million) than in 1988 (0.6 million) (Bean et al., p. 9). Migration accounted for slightly more than 20 percent of this nation's population growth in the 1970s, yet constituted nearly 40 percent of the growth in the decade ending in 1910 (Aleinikoff, p. 60). Recent illegal immigration, of course, adds to the equation. Over 1.2 million deportable aliens, for example, were in the United States in 1984 (Chiswick, p. 13). However, immigration patterns have not been a constant progression. During periods of economic downturns or military struggles, the numbers slowed or stopped. In the 1930s, emigration actually exceeded immigration by 85,000 (Aleinikoff, p. 60). Nor have immigrants been universally welcomed. By the late 1800s, Chinese immigrants in the West were frequently referred to as the "yellow scourge" (Metz, p. 364) or in even more derogatory terms. In the late nineteenth century, citizens of the eastern seaboard feared the loss of national identity as a result of the large number of European arrivals and blamed those immigrants for all manner of vice. Virtually every nationality group has met some opposition initially, and eventually become accepted members of the national community only to have some of their own descendants voice the fear of the dangers to the American union which would result from the addition of foreigners.

Although not universally welcome, immigrants came. The reader can consult the materials listed in the bibliography for a detailed breakdown of the numbers and the countries of origin. The effect of this immigration is that more than 100 million of us can trace an ancestor to someone who entered this country through Ellis Island. Another thirty million of us can identify an ancestor who was brought to this nation on a slave ship. More than twenty-two million of us are of Hispanic origin meaning, of course, that we can trace ancestry to people who reached this country through Spain and Latin America. More than seven million of us claim Asian ancestry and some two million of us can identify an American Indian ancestor.

What Impact Has the Historical Influx of Foreign Language Workers Had Upon the United States Economy?

Not only have immigrants come to live and work in the United States, but in general they (we) prospered. Beyond the numerous individual success stories—such as Joseph Pulitzer, Samuel Gompers, Harry Belafonte, Rose Schneiderman, Judge Joyce Kennard, Owen G. Wang, and Roberto Goizueta—one model of economic development views a continued influx of low wage workers from foreign countries as essential to the productivity and competitiveness of businesses in the United States (Bach in Tucker et al.). This is consistent with the view generally agreed upon by economists and historians that immigration has contributed to overall economic growth in the United States. At the Constitutional Convention, James Madison noted "that part of America which has encouraged [immigrants] most, has advanced most rapidly in population, agriculture and the arts" (Farrand cited in Select Commission on Immigration and Refugee Policy [SCIRP], p. 136). This observation was confirmed more than a century later when the U.S. Bureau of the Census in 1909 concluded that the immigration during the nineteenth century had added thirty million persons to our population and contributed $40 billion to the country's wealth. Those sections of the country where immigrants settled, the report noted, developed into the wealthiest parts of the country whereas those with the smallest proportion of foreign born became the poorest ("A Century of Population Growth" cited in SCIRP, p. 136). In trying to resolve the complex issue of the economic impact of immigration, the 1981 SCIRP staff report summarized the findings and conclusions of a number of economists that immigration, however large, causes substantial economic growth with a beneficial effect on the wages and employment possibilities of other residents. Among the views included was that of W.S. Bernard: "One of the most persistent and recurrent fallacies in popular thought is the notion that immigrants take away the jobs of native Americans. This rests on the misconception that only a fixed number of jobs exist in any economy and that any newcomer threatens the job of any old resident" (SCIRP, p. 73). Julian Simon testified at a Select Commission hearing that "immigrants create jobs as well as take them. They create them by starting new businesses for themselves. They create jobs either directly or indirectly when their goods are exported" (SCIRP, p. 273).

Not all economists, obviously, agree. McCulloch found that while immigrants raise the aggregate income of the American born population, they compete with some American workers whose real wages may be lowered as a result (SCIRP, p. 137). By the late 1970s, the Comptroller General of the United States was reporting that the country had "lost control over its borders" and urged restriction of immigration and the imposition of legal sanctions upon employers for the first time in American history. Testimony offered in favor of federal legislation, which was ultimately adopted in the form of the Immigration Reform and Control Act of 1986 came from individuals and groups, including the president of the National Association for the Advancement of Colored People (NAACP) supporting the notion that the presence of illegal immigrants was syphoning jobs away from lawful United States workers (1986 U. S. Code Cong. and Admin. News 5651). In response, agricultural employers feared the restriction on their labor source would be economically devastating. They proposed and obtained passage of a complicated system calling for legalization of some farm workers already in the country, expansion of an existing temporary worker program to bring in additional farm workers, and a three-year "replenishment program" in the event of a future shortage of immigrant or native workers (Montwieler, p. 66). These competing concerns are reflected in current immigration laws, discussed in Chapter 2 below, with employers often caught in the middle.

It is probably accurate to conclude that the majority of economists and historians agree immigration has historically had a positive impact on this country. It is also accurate to say that there is current concern whether the positive impact will continue. There is probably no way to absolutely resolve this debate. For example, it is relatively easy to identify positive contributions made by immigrants in business, science, government, the arts, and in many other endeavors. More than 30 percent of American Nobel prize winners living in 1981 were immigrants (SCIRP, p. 133). Often children and grandchildren of immigrants make extraordinary contributions. "God Bless America," after all, was written by Irving Berlin, a son of immigrant parents. What will never be known is how many such talents and contributions America has lost due to "restrictive and discriminatory" immigration laws and policies (SCIRP, p. 133).

How Have We Accommodated Non –English-Speaking Workers in the Past?

Throughout the nineteenth century few restrictions were placed on immigration and no legal requirement existed that immigrants know English. Immigrant children in the mid-1800s were looked upon by the public school systems as potential clients to be courted and accommodated to further establish the acceptance of the newly created public school systems (Heath, pp. 12–13). Political leaders urged recruiting these children away from private academies and into the public schools and argued that education of the young would assist parents in making wise political choices. Public school systems recognized the value of multiple languages. In 1870 the U.S. Commissioner of Education concluded that "a knowledge of German is now considered essential to a finished education" (Heath, p. 13). Among the school systems offering instruction in the child's native tongue of bilingual educational programs were Cleveland, St. Louis, and Milwaukee.

By 1890, however, the notion of a publicly funded education system had gained widespread acceptance. The public schools in many areas had filled their classrooms. Further, nativist forces began stirring fears of "the foreign element." Concern began to be expressed over the rising number of immigrants. As a result, recruiting and accommodating immigrant children lost much of its priority. Maintenance of the child's native tongue generally became less important as many schools adopted so-called immersion programs placing immigrant children of many nationalities and tongues immediately into an only-English classroom. One immigrant whose voice was heard on the 1989 P.B.S. presentation *Journey to America* remembered that occasional acts of kindness by individual teachers softened this harsh sink-or-swim approach and the hostility frequently directed by other children against the newcomers.

Legislative proposals began to surface in the late 1800s to establish English ability and literacy as a prerequisite for naturalization (citizenship) of immigrants. President Cleveland vetoed such a proposal in 1895. A requirement that an immigrant possess verbal ability in English as a condition for naturalization became law in 1906. Presidents Taft and Wilson vetoed literacy bills before one finally became law in 1917. However, no law required knowledge of English as a condition of entry into the United States.

For adult workers, English language acquisition was initially largely a function of the availability of immigrant support societies and co-workers. Many immigrants came together with one or more who had acquired English language skills and hired themselves out as a group. These same groups shared information about work, including city transportation systems and employer and union practices. By 1910 the superintendent of the Boston public schools observed that of the estimated thirteen million immigrants in the U.S., three million spoke no English. Yet, in noting that the public schools could not be the sole agent of immigrant education, he warned against forcing language-acquisition programs upon immigrants. "Religious devotion and feeling are inextricably bound up with native language, so that in spite of any intention on our part, when we begin to propose compulsion about language, we probably seem to the foreigner to infringe upon religious rights." Language, he noted, was a "right which even might may not take away . . . a fundamental right which no constitution of men may remove" (Heath, pp. 15, 16).

Immigrants continued to enter this country in large numbers. In fact, the era from the early 1900s through the 1920s represents the years in industrialized America when the percentage and perhaps absolute number of foreign-born workers was at its peak. The concentration of immigrant workers in American cities was dramatic. The 1920 census indicated the following percentage of foreign born in leading industrial cities: New York, 35.4; Boston, 31.9; Cleveland, 30.1; Chicago, 29.8; and Detroit, 29.1. Even more dramatic than the percentage of workers in cities was the percent of foreign born in particular industries. In 1910 immigrant women were represented in the following industries in the following percentages: hemp mills, 75.7; clothing factories, 45.2; and woolen mills, 50. Immigrant males constituted 65.4 percent of the work force in copper mines, 66.8 percent in iron mines, and 46 percent in road construction. Of the males working in clothing factories at that time 75.3 percent were immigrants. Immigrants constituted more than half the work force in the following industries: bakeries, sugar refineries, blast furnaces, leather belt manufacturing, tanneries, copper factories, and woolen mills. They constituted 45.6 percent of the work force in automobile factories. Sixty-four percent of the laborers in slaughter and packing houses were foreign born (Leiserson, pp. 11–15).

This immigrant population was culturally and linguistically diverse. The Immigration Commission examined the demographics of the workers in twenty leading branches of mining and manufacturing in 1910 and reported that more than sixty "races" were represented — including in their categories, "Mexican," "English," "Spanish," "Portuguese," and other groups which would now be referred to in terms of national origin rather than race. It also concluded that the immigrant industrial population was composed mainly of adults who were rarely reached by American public schools, and whose constant association with fellow workers of foreign birth limited their opportunity for socialization with their English speaking American counterparts (Leiserson, p. 17). Some nativist groups viewed the presence of foreigners and foreign workers as a threat. Rioting directed against various national origin groups occurred, and nativists called for more restrictive immigration laws and the expulsion of the foreign born. In responding to concerns about the condition of immigrant workers, George Baer, president of the Philadelphia and Reading Railroad is reported by the AFL-CIO to have replied in 1902, "they don't suffer; they can't even speak English."

However, American industry continued to recognize the value of the immigrant labor pool. The industrial response to a linguistically diverse work force was neither to refuse employment to the foreign born nor to those who spoke a language other than English, nor was the response to prohibit immigrant workers from speaking their own languages on the job. (Contrast this attitude with some contemporary views and situations examined in succeeding chapters of this book.) Rather, American industry realized that immigrant workers were a necessary component of industrial society and that immigrant workers ultimately needed a knowledge of the English language not only for their own benefit but also for the sake of industry. Rather than rely on legislation to make English official and attempt to coerce people into conformity, American industry generally concluded that it, and not government, bore initial responsibility for educating and training its workers, including English instruction. As Harold McCormick of the International Harvester Company stated in 1918:

> A working knowledge of English is as essential to the employee's service as to his citizenship. Without it he cannot be taught to protect himself adequately against exploitation of his ignorance on the outside. Lacking that knowledge, he cannot grasp either the industrial or the social opportunities of his adopted country and must be denied much of the opportunity it offers for self-development. The teaching of English to alien-born employees is, therefore, a primary and fundamental duty resting upon all American employers—a duty whose competent discharge is bound to bring full compensation to all parties and elements in interest. (Leiserson, p. 120)

The YMCA began urging employers to establish English classes at places of employment. The first formal teaching of English to immigrant employees at the place of their employment probably began in 1906 when Harvard students working under the direction of the Cambridge YMCA began teaching classes at the Boston Woven Hose and Rubber Company plant in Cambridge (Leiserson, p. 121).

During the decade following this experiment, the idea took hold in other cities. Classes were organized in 1907 at the Hartford Machine and Screw factory in Hartford, Connecticut and begun in 1910 at the foundry of the Westinghouse Air Brake Company in Pittsburgh. In 1912 the Fall River Cotton Mills began an English program, and in 1913 the Ford English School began conducting a program at its manufacturing plants.

Many of the teaching methods employed in these factories

were developed by Mr. Peter Roberts, a pioneer in the work for the YMCA. The most common method in the factory schools for teaching English began with conversations followed by simple compositions of a few sentences in oral and in written form. Topics were chosen from the work and the habits and necessities of the factory. Substantive learning accompanied the language instruction; health measures, foreman's orders, instructions in manufacturing operations, and the general regulations of the shop were studied.

At the beginning, some employers tried to make attendance at these classes compulsory. The policy aroused resentment and proved to be very unsuccessful. However, the character of the instruction aroused general interest. Employees voluntarily learned English at their own pace and were taught by teachers who respected the diverse cultural backgrounds of the workers. Workers were not encouraged to abandon their own native tongues. Opportunities for advancement to those who learned the English language also proved to be an effective means of securing attendance at these classes.

Meeting times for the factory classes were usually just before and just after the working day. Frequently, the employee would be paid one-half the regular working wage for attendance at the classes.

Language classes were organized at many other industrial plants including the International Harvester Company, Armour and Company, and throughout industrialized areas of the United States.

While industry generally sought to include non-English speaking immigrants in the work force, that is not to say those workers were always welcomed. Derber notes that discrimination against these workers, particularly those who had not yet become citizens, took several forms during the years 1900–1920. First, foremen and management personnel were generally composed of older immigrant groups—Anglo-Saxon, Teutonic, and Irish. They tended to look down upon Eastern and Southern European national origin groups. Second, the labor movement increasingly viewed immigrants as a menace to American jobs—a theme later repeated during the debates which led to the Immigration Reform and Control Act of 1986. The Knights of Labor had opposed Asian immigration and contract European labor after the Civil War. The American Federation of Labor shared these concerns and lobbied for general immigration laws, which ultimately were adopted in 1921 and 1924. Some craft unions excluded non-citizens from membership during this period (Derber, pp. 180–82). Notwithstanding this discrimination, industry generally favored the presence of the new arrivals and sought to accommodate them by making available training, including English language education.

For immigrants working in agriculture, and in particular, for non-European immigrants, the situation was much different, however. Africans who were brought as slaves and their descendants were forbidden to speak their native tongues to one another, reflecting the slaveholders' fear that such communication would conceal plans for rebellion. While slaves were required to communicate in English, they were prohibited from learning to read or write it. Potential teachers were prohibited from teaching them, as Frederick Douglass notes in expressing gratitude to the white children who helped him learn to read:

> I am strongly tempted to give the names of two or three of those little boys, as testimonial of the gratitude and affection I bear them; but prudence forbids; not that it would injure me, but it might embarrass them; for it is almost an unpardonable offence to teach slaves to read in this Christian country. (p. 65)

As Douglass noted, "education and slavery were incompatible with each other" (p. 64). African-Americans who migrated north were generally met with hostility by labor unions (Derber, p. 182). Separate, but inherently unequal, public education became the rule of the land until stricken as unconstitutional by the U.S. Supreme Court in its 1954 decision in *Brown v. Board of Education*.

Asians, who were encouraged to immigrate to provide labor for mining, construction of the railroads, and agriculture met similar disinterest by the American population in their education, yet encountered resentment for maintaining their native tongues. Growing anti-Asian sentiment in 1907 provoked the "Gentlemen's

Agreement," which limited the immigration of Japanese workers. This agreement and the Chinese Exclusion Act, which sought to accomplish what its title suggests, caused a farm labor shortage to begin to develop in the early 1900s.

Unsuccessful attempts by growers to persuade Congress to relax the restrictions upon Asian workers led growers to turn to Mexico in their search for labor (Fuller in Reisler, p. 6). The August 27, 1907 edition of the *California Fruit Grower* told its readers that Mexicans "are plentiful, generally peaceable, and are satisfied with very low social conditions" (ibid.). This market, coupled with the 1910–1917 revolution in Mexico brought large numbers of Mexicans north. Many of them migrated to industrial areas, but the majority remained in agricultural work in the Southwest. Growers repeatedly intervened with the government to assure their labor supply. When rumors surfaced in 1917 that Mexicans would be drafted, for example, growers urged the State Department to quash such rumors, and it did (Reisler, p. 26). Growers also intervened to prevent application of immigration literacy tests to Mexicans. On May 23, 1917, Secretary of Labor Wilson issued a departmental order waiving the test for temporarily admitted Mexican workers (Reisler, p. 27).

No language classes were organized for these laborers. School boards gerrymandered district lines to create separate, generally inadequately funded "Mexican" schools. School boards, many of them dominated by growers, failed to apply compulsory attendance laws to Mexican children. As school officials and growers viewed it, Mexican children belonged in the fields, not the classroom. As a result of their discrimination and poverty, the children of Mexican workers either failed to attend school or, at best, attended intermittently and just at the elementary level (Reisler, p. 141). As a result, no formal efforts were made to instruct either the worker or his or her children in English. Recurring restrictionist pressures, familial contacts in Mexico, and seasonal employment all contributed toward a transient border area Mexican population.

One obvious explanation for the disinterest in educating these workers is that agricultural work required less training than in many industrial settings. Less need seemingly existed for them to acquire English language and other skills. Another explanation is that these workers and their children were the victims of the same educational discrimination aimed at African-American and Asian workers and their families. Apparently, no formal language or other training programs were organized for agricultural workers of these ethnic groups, either. In fact, because skin color was central to the image that white Americans had of these Mexican workers, many of the discriminatory practices whites had established against African-Americans were transferred to the Mexicans. The feeling among many growers was that to maximize output, Mexicans and Blacks were to be treated alike. Few Americans welcomed the Mexican as equals just as few acknowledged the equal humanity of African-Americans or Asians. Reisler cites several comments typical of the 1920s, including former Texas Congressman James Slayden's:

> It is becoming difficult to keep these imported [Mexican] workers on the farms for like the Negroes, they are gregarious, and want to be with their countrymen, and have developed a taste for the movies and the white lights. Equal remuneration will take them all away from the farms and to the city as they never consider the increased cost of living there . . . The average Mexican is as prodigal as the Negro who is, perhaps, the greatest spendthrift in the world. (p. 140)

Mexicans and Mexican-Americans, like their African-American counterparts, were excluded from restaurants and public accommodations, required to ride in the back of buses, and, as decried by the *New York Times* (Sept. 14, 1919; Nov. 16, Nov. 17, 1922), subjected to lynchings (Reisler, p. 142).

The pervasive employment of Mexicans in agriculture, coupled with lack of education, literacy, and English language acquisition, implanted the servile peon image of the Mexican worker in the minds of Americans. Mexican workers of the early part of this century, their families and descendants could then be logically excluded from educational opportunities, work training, and resulting participation in the democratic process. Concern that this type of exclusion could create a permanent underclass was a factor in the U.S. Supreme Court's 1982 decision in the case of *Plyler v.*

Doe, which held unconstitutional a Texas legislative scheme that withheld from local school districts any state funds for the education of children not legally admitted into the U.S. and which also authorized the districts to deny those children enrollment in the public schools.

What Are the Implications of Current Demographics?

Before taking up the legal issues and policy analyses in the chapters to follow, an introduction to some contemporary demographic, sociological, and economic concerns is important. After all, governmental and private sector decision-makers in a democracy and a market economy must be responsive to those concerns.

One question that has conflicting answers is the number of monolingual non-English speakers among us. Despite the concern that the nation has lost control of its borders and that we are being overrun by people who do not know English, the data suggest that the number of people who speak no English at all is relatively small. In 1980 less than one percent (.0057) of the population, or approximately 1.2 million people, spoke no English (1980 U.S Census. 1990 census language figures will not be available until late 1992). This figure might be artificially low given the concern of undercounting among minority groups and the potential reluctance of foreigners here illegally to identify themselves to the census takers. It may be that the efforts of industry, the public schools, and immigration laws requiring competency in English have kept the percentage of monolingual foreign-language speakers low. Or, the market may be at work. If people do, in fact, act in their enlightened self-interest, and if knowledge of English is desirable and helpful in the competition for economic survival, that force may be significant in accounting for the relatively small number of people who do not speak English at all. McGroarty observes that the general power relationship in recent American occupational bilingualism has been for the subordinate group to be non-English speakers who must conform to the language demands of the English-speaking superordinate in order to participate in the economy (p. 162). However, the projections noted earlier (22 percent of new jobs to immigrants in the next two decades), and the anecdotal experiences of employers noted in the *Wall Street Journal* and other articles cited, suggest that accommodating workers who speak no English will remain an issue for some time.

A related issue is whether there is dispersal or concentration of foreign language workers, both in terms of geography and occupational categories. Our historical experience has demonstrated that when an immigrant group possesses a critical mass of economic and social resources, its members may establish for themselves a protected economic sphere revolving around the use of ethnic resources, including language, the social and familial connections of members, and cultural traits that support economic activity (Wilson and Alejandro Portes in McGroarty, p. 162). In a study published in 1988, Chiswick found that illegal immigrants tend to remain in these enclaves. He also found that this phenomenon does not depress wages nor is there a statistically significant relation between duration of residence in an immigrant, ethnic enclave and several established characteristics including the extent to which workers are required at the time of hire to speak English (p. 96). He also concluded that for relatively new immigrants, whether legal or illegal, ethnic enclave employment may serve as an important transitional or "half-way house" function where foreign language fluency is an obviously important skill. His observation is consistent with the historically observed phenomenon that immigrant clustering rather than dispersion is the more typical first pattern, and this concentration has given them additional impact on local labor markets. For non-English speakers, then, the relevance of English to employment depends in part on where they reside. If they reside in an area with many other conationals who speak the same language, they may not need to know English, at least not for initial employment. If the reverse is true, some English will be necessary to acquire a job (McGroarty, p. 163). Since the necessity for occupational bilingualism is partially a function of the potential worker's location, those areas of this country experiencing the greatest influx of immigrants will be the areas where the necessity of accommodating non-English speaking workers will be most profound. From the mid-1970s, 40 percent of all immigrants lived in the ten largest U.S. cities. Immigrants in these cities represent a proportion of the population higher than their share of the U.S. population at large. Between 1970 and 1980, 40 percent of new immigrants settled in either the Los Angeles or New York metropolitan areas with another 20 percent going to one of four other cities: Chicago, San Francisco, Houston, or Miami. The settlement patterns of post-1965 Asian and Latin American immigrants indicate that they are concentrated mainly in Western and Southwestern states although other Spanish speaking groups have demonstrated contemporary residential clustering as well—Puerto Ricans in New York and New Jersey; Cubans in Miami (McGroarty, p. 164).

The final 1990 census, unavailable at this writing, is expected to indicate this same type of clustering in geographic enclaves.

Clustering of non-English speaking workers is not just a function of geography, but also of occupation. Freedman observed that once immigrants enter the United States, their labor market participation is dependent on three factors: how much English they know; the specific occupational skills they already possess; and the nature of the industries where their compatriots already work (Freedman in McGroarty, p. 165). One example of an occupational setting in which the relationship between English language competence and occupation was recently studied is restaurant work. In many large cities, immigrants begin their American employment experience by working in restaurants. At the entry level, English language proficiency is apparently unnecessary for successful completion of many restaurant jobs (dishwasher, busboy) but may be necessary for more skilled positions requiring communication with customers (p. 171). Similar clustering may be expected in entry level occupations, such as agricultural work and construction, where initial training requires little English, or where a sufficient cluster of bilingual workers exists to provide such training and supervision of the non-English speaker. The result of this clustering will be that in geographic areas of high immigrant concentration and in certain occupational categories, the presence of non-English speaking workers will be significant, notwithstanding the overall small percentage of non-English speakers in this country.

Other factors concerning language and job performance are particularly important in considering the Hispanics in the United States. Economists Borjas and Tienda have noted that the great variation in English skills characterizing different national origin groups among Hispanics (Cubans, Puerto Ricans, Mexicans, Central and South Americans) may or may not affect employment depending on local opportunities (McGroarty, p. 170). Other economists have found that the lack of ability to speak English does not significantly affect wages for Hispanic women in the United States (ibid.). Also, linguist Guadalupe Valdes notes that language contact in the border regions between Mexico and the United States is different from the contact that occurs in purely immigrant settings because of the comparable status and range of functions available to each language. While many monolingual members of either group become bilingual, Valdes finds that very little is known why this occurs (McGroarty, p. 175). Although McGroarty indicates no knowledge of specific studies relating bilingualism (English-Spanish) to labor market success along the border, indirect evidence as well as anecdotal information suggests that all other things being equal, bilingualism enhances earning power.

In fact a growing bilingual work force and market likely will be much more significant for language-on-the-job issues than the concerns associated with the relatively few monolingual non-English speakers. The private sector and government, responding to demands from the market and the legal system, will be faced with determinations of whether and how to achieve, maintain, and compensate bilingualism or multilingualism among workers and management. Consider the numbers, particularly those associated with the Spanish language.

In 1985, there were at least 13.2 million Spanish speakers in the United States representing a fourfold increase since 1960 (Macias in W. Connor, p. 287). The Hispanic population in this country has increased from 14.6 million in 1980 to 22.4 million in

1990—a 53 percent increase in one decade. Hispanics in 1990 constituted 9.0 percent of the total U.S. population of 248.7 million (U.S. Dept. of Commerce 1990 Census, released March 11, 1991 CB 91–100). While not all Hispanics speak Spanish, a relatively conservative estimate is that 71 to 75 percent of them have at least some Spanish language ability (comments of U.S. Supreme Court Justice Souter, *Hernandez* case 59 U.S. Law Week 3592, March 5, 1991; Sole, p. 39). If this is accurate, 16.8 million of us spoke at least some Spanish as of 1990.

While large enclaves of Hispanics can be identified in major cities and along the border, the sheer number of Hispanics in this country and the varying occupational opportunities have resulted in dispersal as well. Hispanics constitute more than 10 percent of the population of the states of New Mexico, 38.2; California, 25.8; Texas, 25.5; Arizona, 18.8; Colorado, 12.9; New York, 12.3; Florida, 12.2; and Nevada, 10.4. In terms of numbers, four states count Hispanic populations larger than one million persons: California, 7.7 million; Texas, 4.3 million; New York, 2.2 million; and Florida, 1.6 million. Ten other states, scattered across the country also have Hispanic populations greater than 200,000: Illinois, 904,000; New Jersey, 740,000; Arizona, 689,000; New Mexico, 580,000; Colorado, 424,000; Massachusetts, 288,000; Pennsylvania, 232,000; Washington, 215,000; Connecticut, 213,000; and Michigan, 202,000.

These numbers and projected increases are being reflected in the market place. Two national television networks, Univision and Telemundo, broadcast in Spanish. Univision, founded in 1961, now counts more than five hundred affiliates. Telemundo, which originated in 1986, reaches thirty-seven markets. Spanish-language radio programming and advertising extends across the country, and a policy favoring minority ownership of broadcast facilities has been upheld by the U.S. Supreme Court in the 1989 *Metro Broadcasting* case. Other Spanish-language advertising appears nationwide on billboards, and in newspapers and magazines aimed at the Hispanic consumer whose annual purchasing power was estimated by Telemundo to be $193 billion in 1990. From such evidence it is clear that Spanish will be maintained in this country as an important second language in many contexts (Gaarder in W. Connor, pp. 307–8).

This is not to suggest languages other than Spanish will not be important. Close to 11 percent of the 1980 U.S. population, representing almost twenty-five million people, spoke a language other than English. (1990 Census figures in this regard were not available as of this writing.)

How is the Marketplace Responding to Language-on-the-Job Concerns?

While the legal system wrestles with application of precedent and a weighing of the conflicting legal interests in the adversary arena (Chapters 2–5), there is much evidence that the marketplace is recognizing the need to address language-on-the-job issues. In order to increase the English language competence of its workers, American industry has relearned the successes of the past. Professor Gregory cites the success stories. The Traveler's Insurance Company in Hartford, Connecticut conducts English literacy classes for employees. Many other companies, including Wang Laboratories, Blue Cross and Blue Shield of Massachusetts, ITT in Santa Ana, California, Polaroid Corporation, Planters Peanuts, and Stouffer Foods all have instituted programs offering basic language skills. In fact, the *New York Times* reported on September 8, 1988 that approximately two hundred corporate employers have instituted such programs. On November 7, 1989 the *Wall Street Journal* reported on Motorola's efforts to improve English language skills of its workers. By 1992, the company will have spent up to $30 million on a program which began in 1986 affording basic literacy training in the English language for approximately six thousand workers. Another success story is Pace Foods, Inc. in San Antonio, Texas. The same *Wall Street Journal* article notes that 35 percent of the 250 workers at the plant are Hispanic. To accommodate their bilingualism, staff meetings and employee handbooks are translated into Spanish.

Professional journals are also communicating to management

the need to be sensitive and to accommodate cultural and linguistic differences. In the May-June 1988 edition of *Management World,* Dr. Sondra Thiederman cautiously warns against applying generalities, but notes that some basic education about communication can close the cultural gap that sometimes hurts the performance of foreign-born or foreign-speaking employees. She points out, for example, that among some segments of Asian or Hispanic populations, it would be considered disrespectful and defiant of the supervisor for a worker to begin a task without specific instructions. A manager unfamiliar with this cultural upbringing might erroneously conclude that the worker was lazy or lacked initiative. Another cultural concern is that workers from minority groups might be reluctant to undertake a task for fear of losing face. This *kibun* (Korean) or *hiya* (Tagalog) can be prevented if a manager explains that acting independently is not considered disrespectful. The concern of losing face might also make these employees reluctant, Dr. Thiederman concludes, to admit to not having understood instructions. A manager who observes signs of poor understanding can effectively communicate by using the employee's "cultural language" to explain how management will lose face if tasks are not completed correctly. In a particularly enlightening discussion regarding accent, Dr. Thiederman suggests that the staff as a whole should be made aware that accent is not the equivalent of a lack of education or intelligence. Among her suggestions are that the staff as a whole be taught to be patient but not patronizing, share responsibility for any breakdown of communication, minimize the use of English slang, follow up any questionable conversations with written memos, use non-verbal means of communication, and repeat what has been said if any confusion still exists. The foreign-language speaking employee, she concludes, should be taught the jargon of the industry. He or she should also be made aware that the entire staff accepts responsibility for the success of communication. The foreign-language worker should be encouraged to admit any lack of understanding, to speak slowly and distinctly, and to take a deep breath and start over if he or she is not being understood.

In another article which appeared in the *Journal of Manage-*

ment Development in 1987, John C. Lewis observed that when communicating with people from cultural backgrounds other than our own, we tend to make false assumptions by projecting cognitive similarity. That is, we believe they think the same as we do. The author notes the error of this assumption and, citing Hofstede, shows that culture is the collective mental programming of a people. We tend to see the world the way we were culturally conditioned, the way we learned to see it. Culture in this sense, Hofstede concludes, is slow to change. As a result, he cautions that management techniques and theories that work well in one culture might not be appropriate for others. He examines a recent reorganization undertaken in a Silicon Valley semiconductor company. Team-building workshops were considered successful in building trust and interpersonal relations between workers from different cultural backgrounds. He suggests there will be a growing need for such cultural awareness training for both the local and foreign born so they can understand, cope with, and manage the differences that will continue to arise in companies employing a multinational work force in high technology jobs. Without wishing to create stereotypical over-generalizations, he notes that managers from Japan and Middle Eastern countries tend to enter negotiating sessions at a pace different from Americans and Europeans. They have a higher need for testing conditions, establishing trust, and developing relationships before getting down to business. American managers, as well as many Western Europeans believe that content takes precedence, and for them importance is attached to crisp negotiations and decisions and keeping to a schedule. Such variances leave managers bewildered as to why their styles, which appear to be very rational and appropriate to them, are not effective in other countries and cultures. Similarly, a 1986 article in the *Training and Development Journal* notes the need for both foreign and American management and employees to be sensitive to the influence of language and ethnic culture on communication, performance, interpersonal skills, and working relationships. Among the training strategies suggested by the authors to impart sensitivity to cultural and language issues are to create a program for the systematic examination of English language problems, coupled with intensive language awareness and improvement training for minority language employees.

However, despite these enlightened management strategies, no uniform agreement exists regarding the value of developing multilingualism in the American work force. Lambert notes that numerous surveys conclude that American companies, even those with numerous foreign transactions, place foreign language competence close to the bottom in their list of desiderata in hiring new employees. While chief executive officers will generally agree that businesses should cosmopolitanize its executive core and increase its foreign language competence, this does not seem to translate into individual corporate policy. However, in the same article, he reports the results of a survey showing that 41 percent of the respondents who had foreign language skills reported that it was an important or very important factor in securing a job. In another article focusing on American businessmen in Japan, Cramer found that while American companies in general look for business acumen and interest before Japanese language ability in recruitment, the combination of business skills and Japanese language fluency does seem to be preferred (p. 93).

Clifford and Fischer note the great need of the federal government for foreign language competence. They conclude that consideration should be given to reducing our national linguistic isolation by providing a general introduction to world languages and cultures (p. 120).

In fact, encouragement of functional bilingualism may become critical for our economic survival. As the European community consolidates its economic relations, it is becoming increasingly obvious to political and business leaders in Great Britain that additional language skills need to be developed. On May 23, 1990 the *London Daily Telegraph,* quoting the Prince of Wales, noted that Britain will become a peripheral and insignificant trading nation if it continues to neglect the importance of learning foreign languages. With the single European market and a unified Germany, the Prince told education and business leaders that Britain could not afford further mistakes. One month previously, tourism workers in Britain were warned to brush up on foreign languages or risk the demise of their businesses in the face of stiff European competition. Competition with a unified European market will undoubtedly impact the United States. So, too, will increased commercial ties with Japan.

In Tokyo, President Bush noted the economic importance of language in our trade relations: "I want the people of our countries to have a better understanding of one another. We need more Americans who can speak Japanese and who understand the workings of the Japanese marketplace" (*New York Times*, January 8, 1992, § A, p. 1). A proposed trade agreement with Mexico, being negotiated as this book is written, will, if completed, require the immediate availability of people with Spanish as well as English language skills to perform an infinite number of transactions in furtherance of the treaty. In broad terms, the treaty would remove trade barriers between the United States and Mexico, leaving American concerns free to move material, operations, and employees across the border. Mexico would be given reciprocal rights. All of the functions of industry from contractual negotiations to employment and job training would undoubtedly fall to those companies whose representatives were bilingual. Under this set of circumstances, no law or sets of laws will be necessary to require tolerance or acceptance of foreign language skills; the economic incentive for bilingualism will, at least in the border regions, make the enforcement of restrictive language policies too inefficient and hinder competition. Even as the treaty is negotiated, demographics and the marketplace may quickly relegate restrictive language policies to the status of a historical oddity.

Similarly, Professor Gregory notes the impact immigration and language diversity are likely to have on union organization:

> Perceptive unions are implementing strategies to reach out to organize prospective new union members. Given the rapidly changing demographics of the current and future work force, workers whose primary language is not English are an important and growing potential union constituency, particularly in burgeoning service industries. Therefore, the more capable the union's programs in anticipating and meeting the needs of linguistically heterogeneous workers, the better the union will be able to organize and serve these new members. Additionally, union leadership with multilingual

capabilities will be best able to identify and develop future union leaders from within the rank and file and thus be better able to meet future challenges.

Finally, a growing translation industry is surfacing in this country, in response to industry's language needs. A trade group consisting of over three thousand members has organized itself into the American Translators Association. A survey in 1988 indicates that over half of the members have earned master's or doctorate degrees and 91 percent have completed four years of college. A November 8, 1987 article in the *Chicago Tribune* notes that in addition to the traditional publishing houses, government agencies, and trade associations which have long used translators, high tech firms, advertising agencies, and the film industry are among the many segments of the business community now hiring translators. The economic advantages to those with multiple language skills was noted in a June 30, 1989 story in the *Los Angeles Times*:

> Increasingly in this multilingual city, learning a second or third language is becoming an advantage if not a necessity. The practicalities of doing business in an international capital, as well as the simple desire to communicate with new neighbors from Latin America and Asia is fueling a surge in the popularity of foreign languages in Los Angeles . . . . The Los Angeles phenomenon is part of a burgeoning national movement, spurred by the desire to make the country more competitive, according to experts in the field . . . The translating and interpreting business, meanwhile, is booming, with the ranks of court interpreters almost doubling each year, according to leaders in that field.

This recognition by industry in Los Angeles of the economic benefits to be gained by linguistic accommodation was illustrated to this author during a July 1991 visit. The Anaheim Sheraton Hotel employs customer service representatives fluent in many languages. Many businesses, including Disneyland, provide the services of multilingual personnel. There is apparently a profit to be made by this accommodation.

Another market response to the need for multilingualism is the developing industry of machine translation. According to the

November 20, 1989 edition of the *San Diego Business Journal,* Systran Translation Systems, Inc., formed in 1968, uses computers to translate a dozen languages for private and governmental clients. The Systran software translates one page of text in about two minutes depending upon the computer. It does not translate word for word but rather translates a section of a text at a time, with an accuracy rate of about 80 percent. A human editor then reviews and corrects the computer-generated translation.

A development with dramatic implications regarding language-on-the-job issues is the creation of computer software offering immediate language translation. One such program is MicroT's program, "Spanish Assistant." In this author's "Law and Language" course conducted at Texas Tech University in the fall of 1990, one student, Mr. Dale Rose (J.D. Texas Tech 1991) demonstrated the program. While it was not 100 percent accurate and while a working knowledge of the Spanish language was necessary to answer the questions posed by the program regarding the selection of verbs, tenses, and other factors, the demonstration indicated that language translation software is now available for personal computer use and will undoubtedly become more sophisticated in the future.

In fact, technological advances may eventually make the entire consideration of language-on-the-job issues obsolete. Imagine the scenario where at some time in the not-too-distant future workers, managers, and customers of every language background can communicate virtually instantaneously by means of individual computers built into headphones. The speaker's language would be immediately translated verbally into the listener's language. Even colloquialisms and regional accents could be programmed into the computer depending upon the listener's preference.

Since the technology to resolve language issues is not yet available, this science fiction scenario will have to wait. In the meantime, every indication is that industry and the courts will have to grapple with these issues. A more detailed examination of the historical, sociological, and demographic concerns which frame the background of current language-on-the-job issues can be found in the bibliography following this chapter. With this background, we turn next to a consideration of how the legal system is responding to these concerns.

Bibliography

Books

1. Thomas Aleinikoff & David Martin, *Immigration Process and Policy* (1985).

2. Frank D. Bean, Jurgen Schmandt, Sidney Weintraub, eds., *Mexican and Central American Population and U.S. Immigration Policy* (1989).

3. D. Bruckner, ed., *Politics and Language: Spanish and English in the United States* (1978).

4. Barry Chiswick, *Illegal Aliens: Their Employment and Employers* (1988).

5. Walker Connor, ed., *Mexican-Americans In Comparative Perspect-t ive* (1985).

6. Milton Derber, *The American Idea of Industrial Democracy* 1865–1965 (1970).

7. Frederick Douglass, *Narrative of the Life of Frederick Douglass, An American Slave* (1969).

8. Charles A. Ferguson, Shirley Brice Heath, eds., *Language in the USA* (1981).

9. William Leiserson, *Adjusting Immigrant and Industry* (1969).

10. Leon Metz, *Border* (1989).

11. Nancy Humel Montwieler, *The Immigration Reform Law of 1986* (1987).

12. Bill Piatt, ¿ *Only English? Law and Language Policy in the United States* (1990).

13. Mark Reisler, *By the Sweat of Their Brow: Mexican Immigrant Labor in the United States* (1976).

14. Robert Tucker, Charles B. Keely, Linda Wrigley, eds., *Immigration and U.S. Foreign Policy* (1990).

Articles

1. Irene Chang, *U.S. Supports Nurse in English-Only Suit*, L.A. Times, April 3, 1990, at B3.

2. Roy T. Clifford & Donald C. Fischer, Jr., *Foreign Language Needs in the U.S. Government*, 511 Annals of Am. Academy of Pol. & Soc. Sci. 109 (Sept. 1990).

3. Bernice A. Cramer, *Developing Competitive Skill: How American Business People Learn Japanese*, 511 Annals of Am. Academy of Pol. & Soc. Sci. 85 (Sept. 1990).

4. Sarah Henry, *Fighting Words*, L.A. Times Mag., June 10, 1991, at 10.

5. Marita Hernandez, *Second Languages: Cultural Mix Translates into a Boom*, L.A. Times (Friday, Home ed.), June 30, 1989.

6. Carol Kleiman, *Business Spreads the Word About Good Translators*, Chicago Tribune Co. (Sunday, Final ed., Jobs Sec.), Nov. 8, 1987.

7. Joel Kofkin, *Fear and Reality in the Los Angeles Melting Pot*, L.A. Times Mag., Nov. 5, 1989, at 6.

8. Richard D. Lambert, *Foreign Language Use Among International Business Graduates*, 511 Annals of Am. Academy of Pol. & Soc. Sci. 47 (Sept. 1990).

9. Christina Lee, *As Nations Expand their Diplomatic and Trading Borders, The Need for Sensitive and Intelligent Translation and Interpretation Mushrooms*, L.A. Times (Sunday, Orange County ed., Bus. Sec. (June 3, 1990)).

10. John C. Lewis, *Issues Concerning High Technology Managers from Multiple Cultural Backgrounds*, 6 Jrnl. of Mgmt. Development (UK) No. 3, 1987, p. 73.

11. Paul Marston, *Prince Calls for More Foreign Language Skills,* The Daily Telegraph (London) May 24, 1990 at sec. 2.

12. Bob Masterson & Bob Murphy, *Internal Cross-Cultural Management*, 40 Training and Development Journal, April 1986, p. 56.

13. Mary E. McGroarty, *Bilingualism in the Workplace*, 511 Annals of Am. Academy of Pol. & Soc. Sci. 159 (Sept. 1990).

14. Ann Middleton, *Systran Takes Translation Software to New Market*, San Diego Business Journal, November 20, 1989, § 1 at 9.

15. Seth Mydans, *Pressure for English-Only Job Rules Stirring a Sharp Debate Across the U.S.*, N.Y. Times, Aug. 8, 1990, at A12.

16. Patricia Newman, *Profile of the American Translator*, Languages at Crossroads: Proceedings of the 29th Annual American Translators Association Conference (D. Hammond ed. 1988).

17. Note, *Undocumented Aliens: Education, Employment and Welfare in the United States and New Mexico*, 9 N.M.L. Rev. 99 (1978).

18. James E. Pearce & Jeffrey W. Gunther, *Illegal Immigration From Mexico: Effects on the Texas Economy*, 6 Sw. J. of Bus. & Econ. 28 (Winter-Spring 1989).

19. Bill Piatt, *Born as Second Class Citizens in the U.S.A.: Children of Undocumented Parents*, 63 Notre Dame L. Rev. 35 (1988).

20. Project, *Developments in the Law: Immigration Policy and the Rights of Aliens*, 96 Harv. L. Rev. 1286 (1983).

21. *Report Cites Hispanics' Woes*, The Dallas Morning News, April 11, 1991, at 10A

22. Jolie Solomon, *Times Grapple with Language Barriers*, Wall St. J., Nov. 7, 1989.

23. Sondra Thiederman, *Breaking through to Foreign-Born Employees*, 17 Management World No. 3, May/June 1988, p. 23.

24. Tourism Workers Warned, "Learn a Language", Pres. Home News, Press A. Newsfile (England), (February 28, 1990).

25. Michael Wines, *Japanese Visit on the Surface: Jovial Bush, Friendly Crowds,* The New York Times, January 8, 1992, at A1.

Statutes

1. Act of Feb. 5, 1917, 39 Stat. 874 (Immigration law literacy requirements).

2. Chinese Exclusion Act of 1882, ch. 126, 22 Stat. 58 (1882).

3. Immigration Reform & Control Act of 1986, Pub. L. No. 99-603, 100 Stat. 3359 (codified as amended in scattered sections of 7 U.S.C., 8 U.S.C., 18 U.S.C., 20 U.S.C., 29 U.S.C., & 42 U.S.C.) (1986); Pub. L. No. 100–203, 101 Stat. 1330 (current version at 42 U.S.C. §673) (1987).

Cases

1. *Brown v. Board of Education*, 349 U.S. 294 (1954).

2. *Chae Chan Ping v. United States* ("Chinese Exclusion Case"), 130 U.S. 581 (1889).

3. *Metro Broadcasting Inc. v. F.C.C.*, 110 S. Ct. 1467 (1990).

4. *Plyler v. Doe*, 457 U.S. 202 (1982).

5. *Shin v. INS*, 750 F.2d 122, 130 (D.C. Cir. 1984), (dissent of Justice Starr re: loss of control over borders).

Other Authorities

1. Bureau of the Census, U.S. Dept. of Commerce, *Statistical Abstract of the United States* 34 (1986).

2. Hudson Institute Study, cited in David Gregory, *Union Leadership and Workers' Voices: Meeting the Needs of Linguistically Heterogeneous Union Members*, 58 Cinc. L. Rev. 115, 128 (1989).

3. *Journey to America*, (P.B.S. documentary 1989).

4. Observations of Justice Souter, *Hernandez v. New York*, re: percentage of Spanish-speaking Latinos, 59 U.S. L.W. 3592 (March 5, 1991).

5. Report to the Congress by the Comptroller General of the United States, *Illegal Entry at U.S.-Mexican Borders: 7 Multiagency Enforcement Efforts Have Not Been Effective in Stemming the Flow of Drugs and People* (1977).

6. Select Commission on Immigration and Refugee Policy, Staff Report: *U.S. Immigration Policy and the National Interest* (April 30, 1981).

7. U.S. Dept. of Commerce News: *Census Bureau Completes Distribution of 1990 Redistricting Tabulations to States*, Release CB91–100 and accompanying tables (March 11, 1991).

8. U.S. Govt. Accounting Office Report to the Congress, *ImmigrationReform: Employer Sanctions and the Question of Discrimination*, GAO/66D–90–62 (March 1990).

9. 1980 U.S. Census, tables 183 (U.S. Summary 1–181 and 1–182), and 256 (U.S. Summary 1–16).

10. 1986 U.S. Code Cong. & Admin. News 5649.

Part Two

THE LAW APPLIED
AND CRITIQUED

CHAPTER TWO

LANGUAGE AND HIRING, PROMOTION, AND RETENTION DECISIONS

As is evident in Chapter 1, language is going to be an important concern in decisions concerning hiring, promotion, and retention as a result of immigration and growth in our Hispanic and Asian populations. The experiences of employers and employees, as noted in academic journals, popular media, and the courts bear out this observation. The decision whether to employ someone with limited English skills or who has an accent carries with it many economic, legal, and moral implications. We take up these issues in this chapter by discussing the judicial application of three relevant federal statutes. State statutes and local human rights ordinances might also be relevant, but the national acts provide the most important legal framework in these areas. We will consider in particular recent studies and cases concerning English spoken with an accent. We will also examine dilemmas facing employers and employees as a result of these strictures.

Before beginning our examination of the applicable statutes and cases, however, a brief introduction is needed to outline the difficulty courts and legislatures demonstrate when dealing with language issues. While the workforce and market may change relatively quickly, the development of jurisprudence follows, or in many cases, lags. Development of applicable principles is inconsistent, reflecting societal ambivalence about accommodating other tongues and their speakers and reflecting the confusion of monolingual judges and legislators over the very nature of language itself. When language becomes a factor in judicial determinations, it appears under the categories of race or national origin.

Rather than focusing on the impact on underlying interests, courts bog down trying to force language issues into the narrow pigeon-holes of the race or national origin of its users.

With these preliminary caveats in mind, we turn now to discussing the statutes and cases regarding the use of language in hiring, promotion, and retention matters. With an understanding of what the law is, and with some critiques of its applications, we will return in Chapter 6 with a comprehensive discussion of what it should be.

Equal Employment Opportunity Act

Title VII of the Civil Rights Act of 1964, 42 U.S.C. §2000e-§2000e–17 (Equal Employment Opportunity Act) prohibits employment discrimination on the basis of race, color, religion, sex, or national origin. It was intended to assure equality of employment opportunities, eradicate discrimination in employment, and provide remedies to make the victims of discrimination whole. Prohibited discrimination is not limited to discrimination in hiring, firing, or the payment of wages, but includes discriminatory terms and conditions of employment. Title VII applies to employers with fifteen or more employees. It prohibits not only intentional discrimination with respect to conditions of employment, but also applies to facially neutral rules that have a disparate impact on protected groups of workers. The Equal Employment Opportunity Commission (EEOC), an administrative body created by the Act, is charged with enforcing it. The Act is complex and its history fascinating. (The best single source for understanding its history and application is the treatise by Professor Rossein cited in the bibliography of this chapter.)

Although Title VII prohibits discrimination on the basis of "national origin," the Act does not define the term. Legislative history indicates that the term was understood to mean the country from which a person or the person's forebears came. In fact, Congress deleted the word "ancestry" from the final version of the act because it considered the term synonymous with national origin. In 1973, the United States Supreme Court stated that national origin "on its face refers to the country where a person was born, or more broadly, the country from which his or her ancestors came" (*Espinoza* case).

Although Title VII does not explicitly mention language discrimination and, notwithstanding that the Act does not explicitly authorize the EEOC to issue interpretive guidelines, in 1970 the EEOC published the first "Guidelines on Discrimination Because of National Origin" (29 C.F.R. §1606.1 (1971)). These guidelines made it clear that the EEOC intended to eliminate covert as well as overt practices of discrimination where persons had been denied equal employment opportunity for reasons grounded in national origin considerations. Among the practices the EEOC concluded could be examples of impermissible national origin discrimination on the basis of language was the "use of tests in the English language where the individual came from circumstances where English was not that person's first language or mother tongue, and where English language skill is not a requirement of the work to be performed" (29 C.F.R. §1606.1(b)). In general, the United States Supreme Court has upheld the authority of the EEOC to issue such guidelines and affords them deference (*Griggs* case, 401 U.S. at 433–434).

Specifically in the language context, the Supreme Court has recognized that refusal to hire on the basis of language can constitute national origin discrimination (*Espinoza* case, 414 U.S. 86, 92, n.5 (1973)). Other cases following the guide of the EEOC and the Supreme Court have also reached the same conclusion (*Jones v. United Gas*). More recently, in 1987, the EEOC issued additional guidelines (some of which are discussed in Chapter 3 of this book in the context of speak English rules), making it explicit that "an individual's primary language is an essential characteristic of national origin" (29 C.F.R. §1606.7 (1987)).

There is some concern that using this national origin pigeonhole to protect the rights of speakers of languages other than English is analytically unsound and taps into nativist fears of things foreign (see Chapter 6). However, it is now well accepted by both the EEOC and the courts that unjustifiable language restrictions in hiring and retention decisions can constitute impermissible national origin discrimination under Title VII.

Some cases illustrate this position. In 1969, the EEOC determined that reasonable cause existed to believe that an employer violated the Equal Employment Opportunity Act when a new branch manager of a printing facility fired a typesetter for alleged incompetency on the basis of a language problem. The new branch manager identified the reason for the firing as the employee "not being able to speak, read, and understand English very well" (2 Fair Empl. Prac. Cas. (BNA) Number YAU 9-048 at 78). The difficulty with the employer's position from the viewpoint of the EEOC was that the typesetter had acquired more than sixteen years experience as a typesetter, implicitly demonstrating the ability to communicate effectively in English as of the time of his firing by a new branch manager in January 1968.

This protection against discrimination based upon foreign language ability even extends to protect from adverse employment decisions persons whose foreign accent does not interfere with their ability to perform duties. This principle was set down in a 1974 case decided by the U. S. Circuit Court of Appeals for the Tenth Circuit, in a case entitled *Carino v. University of Oklahoma Board of Regents*. In that case, Mr. Carino was hired by the defendants as supervisor of a dental laboratory at the University of Oklahoma College of Dentistry. The Court found that Mr. Carino's demotion from these duties resulted from the opinion held by certain dental college faculty that the plaintiff was unsuitable to continue as supervisor because of his national origin (Republic of the Philippines) and his related accent. Because it was not proven that his accent interfered with his duties, the Court concluded that a showing had been made of unlawful national origin discrimination.

In 1980 the U.S. Circuit Court of Appeals for the Sixth Circuit upheld the finding of a U.S. District Court that an employee of the Ohio Department of Public Welfare had been the victim of unlawful discrimination when she was denied two promotions based upon her accent. In that case the plaintiff, Rozalia Berke, was born in Poland, emigrated to England at the age of 21, and eventually moved to Ohio. She had earned bachelor of arts and master of arts degrees from the University of Cincinnati, but still retained an accent.

In 1983, an Oregon welfare worker by the name of Louiseau was denied a promotion because co-workers and supervisors reacted negatively to his French West Indian accent. At trial, the U.S. District Court for Oregon found he was the victim of national origin discrimination.

In a 1984 case, a U.S. District Court in North Carolina agreed with a New Zealand-born plaintiff that if he could prove he had been discriminated against by his employer because of his accent, such would constitute national origin discrimination. However, the employer denied ridiculing the accent and the Court found that in any event plaintiff had not shown any specific discriminatory conduct attached to the remarks.

However, neither Title VII nor the cases which apply it stand for a broad proposition that no employer may ever decline to offer employment or promotions to someone with limited English ability. Language difficulties that interfere with the performance of duties may legitimately be considered in employment decisions. In 1978, for example, a decision of the U. S. District Court for the Southern District of New York (*Mejia v. New York Sheraton Hotel*) concluded that the New York Sheraton Hotel did not act in a discriminatory manner when a Hispanic woman was denied a position as a front office cashier. The Court upheld the hotel's contention that a cashier's ability to communicate effectively in English was a necessity of the business, because the position would necessarily bring the worker in contact and communication with the guests of the hotel. At the trial of the case, the Court noted that the woman's English language deficiencies in her testimonial responses made it difficult for the Court, the reporter, and counsel to understand what she was saying. These same deficiencies apparently had not prevented her from performing her previous duties effectively as a chamber maid where English language skills were not as important.

In a 1983 case a Chinese American associate professor was denied a promotion after his committee concluded that his accent limited his classroom effectiveness and resulted in only average teaching ability. The U.S. District Court for the Western District of Pennsylvania upheld the denial, finding the accent determination comments were directed to the legitimate issue of teaching effectiveness.

A 1989 decision by the U.S. Ninth Circuit Court of Appeals upheld an employer's decision not to hire a worker whose accent, the employer concluded, would have a deleterious effect upon job performance. This case appears to be an important harbinger of future approaches to language discrimination cases and merits a detailed examination.

In the case, Manuel T. Fragante was denied a post as a clerk with the Honolulu Department of Motor Vehicles because of his Filipino accent, notwithstanding that he had scored first out of 721 applicants on the written exam for the job. The opinion of the U.S. District Court of Hawaii provides additional factual background. The Court determined that Mr. Fragante, a U.S. citizen, was born in the Philippines in 1921. He was well educated, with honors, in the Philippines. He served as a career officer for thirty years in the Philippines Armed Forces and retired while holding the position of Army Adjutant. Most of Mr. Fragante's schooling, both civilian and military, was conducted primarily in English. After retirement he had subsequent supervisory and administrative work experience in Manila, the Philippines.

In April 1981 he and his wife immigrated to the United States. He was naturalized as a citizen in Honolulu, Hawaii in January 1983.

In November 1981, Mr. Fragante responded to an ad and applied for a position as a clerk with the Honolulu Department of Motor Vehicles. After ranking first of 721 on a written test, he was certified along with fourteen others as eligible for the position. He ranked first among those eligible. In April 1982 Mr. Fragante interviewed for the position. Two interviewers talked to him for approximately ten to fifteen minutes. The Court found that the interview was informal. No written interview questions were prepared, but it was standard as compared to other interviews then and on previous vacancies. Although standard, the interview lacked formality as to standards, instructions, guidelines, or criteria for its conduct. There was no validation of questions, and the interviewers were not formally trained in the process.

After the interview, on the same day, the interviewers scored Fragante on an interview rating sheet. The rating sheet, the Court found, was inadequate. Ratings categories were vague, qualitative in nature though reduced to quantitative terms, non-correlative, and not clearly job related nor well defined. Dr. James Kirkpatrick, an industrial psychologist, termed it seriously flawed. He testified that written tests in general are acceptable and reliable, but that the interview and rating system applied to Fragante were entirely subjective and did not meet federal or any acceptable standards of collective decision making.

After all interviews were completed, Fragante was notified that because of his accent he was not selected for the job:

> As to the reason for your non-selection, we felt the two selected applicants were both superior in their verbal communication ability. As we indicated in your interview, our clerks are constantly dealing with the public and the ability to speak clearly is one of the most important skills required for the position. Therefore, while we were impressed with your educational and employment history, we felt the applicants selected would be better able to work in our office because of their communication skills. (699 F. Supp. at 1431)

Fragante filed suit, alleging national origin discrimination under Title VII and race discrimination under 42 U.S.C. §1981 (discussed in the next section). In dismissing the suit, the Court went on to note that the job Fragante applied for is a difficult one because it involves dealing with a great number of disgruntled members of the public. The clerk must deal with two hundred to five hundred people per day, many of whom are angry or complaining and who do not want to hear what the clerk may have to explain concerning their applications or in answer to their questions. It is a high turnover position where people leave quickly because of the stress involving daily contact with contentious people. The Court found that listeners stop listening to Filipino accents, resulting in a breakdown of communications. Just as in the 1978 New York case, the Court then went on to note that the plaintiff had a different manner of pronunciation and that he would often not respond directly to the questions as propounded in court. Curiously, the Court found that Fragante maintained much of his military bearing.

From these facts the Court concluded:

> The requirement of being able to communicate clearly and effectively with an often contentious general public is a bona fide occupational qualification which is necessary to the City's business of providing services and assistance to the general public concerning motor vehicles and licensing matters.

> The results of Plaintiff's interview show that his oral communication skills were hampered by his accent or manner of speaking, and pronouncing, which made it difficult for the City interviewers to understand him.

> In spite of the insufficiencies of the rating system and the weaknesses of the interview process, as applied to the Plaintiff, they were not discriminating. Nor did the interviewers utilize them in any way to discriminate against the Plaintiff. (699 F.Supp. at 1432)

Fragante appealed this decision to the U.S. Ninth Circuit Court of Appeals. He was not successful. The appellate court determined that the record conclusively showed that he was passed over because of the deleterious effect of his Filipino accent on his ability to communicate orally, not merely because he had such an accent (888 F.2d at 599). However, Fragante may have won a victory for future victims of accent discrimination in that the Ninth Circuit opinion contains this caution:

> Accent and national origin are obviously inextricably intertwined in many cases. It would therefore be an easy refuge in this context for an employer unlawfully discriminating against someone based on national origin to state falsely that it was not the person's national origin that caused the employment or promotion problem, but the candidate's inability to measure up to the communications skills demanded by the job. We encourage a very searching look by the district courts at such a claim. (888 F.2d at 596)

Obviously, not everyone was satisfied with the *Fragante* decision. One legal scholar, Matsuda, reviewed the trial transcript. One of the witnesses who testified at trial was Dr. Michael Forman, a linguist who specializes in interactions between English and Filipino speakers. Matsuda noted that Forman testified that Mr. Fragante spoke grammatically correct, standard English, with the characteristic accent of someone raised in the Philippines. There is a history, in Hawaii and elsewhere, of prejudice against this accent, the linguist explained, which causes some listeners to "turn off" and not comprehend it. But the degree of phonological deviation in Fragante's speech was not so far afield from other accents of English-speakers in Hawaii that he would not be understood. Any nonprejudiced speaker of English would have had no trouble understanding Mr. Fragante, Forman concluded.

Matsuda notes that among the ironies Dr. Forman observed during the proceedings was that attorneys for both sides suffered lapses in grammar and sentence structure, as did the judge. Mr. Fragante's English, a review of the transcript confirmed, was more nearly perfect in standard grammar and syntax than any other speaker in the courtroom. Mr. Fragante testified for two days, under the stress of both direct and cross-examination. The judge and the examiners spoke to Fragante in English and understood his answers. A court reporter understood and took down his words verbatim. In the functional context of the trial, everyone understood Manuel Fragante's speech. Lawyers for both sides, as well as the defendant's witnesses, spoke with accents. Nonetheless, Fragante lost his appeal, and with it the chance to occupy the position as a clerk, which was the lowest paying job of the city/county of Honolulu.

Another "accent" case, also originating in the U.S. District Court for Hawaii involved an applicant for a position as a Weather Service specialist. In that case, *Kahakua v. Hallgrem*, the plaintiff was a Hawaiian employed by the Honolulu Weather Service Forecast office as a Communications Specialist. When he was denied a promotion to the Weather Service Specialist post, and a Caucasian was selected in his place, he sued. In rejecting his claim, the District judge noted that the white candidate had better diction, enunciation, pronunciation, cadence, intonation, voice clarity, and understandability. The Court noted that there was no racial or physiological reason why Kahakua could not have used standard English pronunciations. The judge chose not to adopt the conclusion of a linguist who testified that Kahakua's Hawaiian-Creole pronunciation was not incorrect, but was rather one of the many varieties of pronunciation of standard English. On appeal, the Ninth Circuit affirmed.

Matsuda takes issue with this case as well. In her thought-provoking article "Voices of America: Accent, Antidiscrimination Law and a Jurisprudence for the Last Reconstruction," published in the March 1991 *Yale Law Journal,* she cites recent animosity against people with "accents". She notes that an October 18, 1988 editorial in the *San Jose Mercury News* recommended voting against a Korean-American candidate for city council because of his accent. She identifies many other instances of conscious and unconscious discrimination based upon accent. Ironically, she notes, everyone has an accent, even the deaf who use sign language to communicate. Matsuda's article, articulate and passionate, is critical of the *Fragante/Kahakua* analysis. Those cases, however, will undoubtedly help shape the approaches of courts to foreign language discrimination cases under Title VII.

One of the areas likely to involve recurring accent issues is the teaching profession. House Bill 638 (May 28, 1989) of the Texas Legislature requires each state institution of higher education to establish a program or short course to assist certain nonnative English-speaking faculty members to become proficient in English. While no one would quarrel with the need to have teachers competent in English, this legislation appears to be the product of concerns voiced in Texas and in other states regarding professors and teachers with "foreign" accents. In implementing this legislation, this author's employer, Texas Tech University adopted a policy of providing that "all (new) faculty interviews shall include an oral proficiency evaluation which includes information on pronunciation, fluency, vocabulary, grammar, intonation and general comprehensibility of the faculty member being interviewed." Additional assessments apply to "non-native English speaking" faculty. Currently employed "non-native English speaking faculty" are required to be certified as competent in the English language. As a member of the Faculty Senate, this author cast one of only a few "no" votes when the scheme was presented to our Senate for ratification.

Before leaving a discussion of language discrimination under Title VII, it may be useful to briefly discuss the way such cases may be brought in the future and, applying what can be gleaned from the current status of the law, help employers and employees predict the treatment these cases will receive under Title VII.

Under both Title VII and EEOC guidelines, two theories exist by which potential employees can show unlawful national origin discrimination: disparate treatment and disparate impact. Disparate treatment cases involve a showing of intentional discrimination against a member of a protected class. Once the *prima facie* case of discrimination is made by the plaintiff, the burden of production of evidence then shifts to the employer or defendant to articulate a legitimate, nondiscriminatory reason for its action. Even if the defendant comes forward with a reason, the plaintiff has the opportunity to show that the reason is a pretext. That is, the plaintiff can show that the proffered reason is not true, or is a mask or a cover for discrimination. Along these lines, a rule or practice adopted for the *purpose* of discriminating against a protected class violates Title VII unless it meets a strict bona fide occupational qualification (BFOQ) test. The burden of persuasion remains with the employee throughout a disparate treatment case (Rossein, pp. 2–4, 2–5).

Fragante was a disparate treatment case. His prima facie case consisted of a showing that he was qualified, and yet the position he sought was purposely given to someone else because of his accent. The defendant articulated the communication problem with disgruntled citizens as a legitimate reason for its action. Fragante was not able to rebut by convincing the Court that this reason was not true, or that it was a mask for discrimination. The Court found the communication ability to be a BFOQ.

The other way in which a plaintiff can show unlawful discrimination is the disparate impact case. Under this theory, the tradition was that a rule that appeared facially neutral but which nonetheless fell more harshly upon a protected group violated Title VII unless the employer could justify it by carrying the burden of persuasion by showing a business necessity for it *(Griggs* case). In the 1978 *Mejia* case, the employer demonstrated that a cashier's ability to communicate in English was a business necessity.

For a brief time, as a result of the 1989 decision of the U.S. Supreme Court in the *Wards Cove* case, the employer's burden was lessened. In that case, the defendant companies operated salmon canneries in Alaska. Cannery line jobs were unskilled positions filled seasonally with predominantly minority workers, while higher paying noncannery positions were filled with predominantly white workers. Dormitory and mess hall facilities were separate for both categories of workers, with the noncannery workers receiving better accomodations. Nonwhite cannery workers sued. They alleged the racial stratification of the work force was caused by the companies' hiring and promotion policies. Ultimately, on appeal to the United States Supreme Court, the companies prevailed. The Court held that racial imbalance alone does not make a prima facie disparate impact case. Further, even if an employee made a prima facie showing, the employer needed only to produce evidence to show a business justification for the challenged practice.

"Business justification" under *Wards Cove* consisted of evidence that the challenged practice served in a significant way the legitimate employment goals of the employer. The employer did not have to show that the practice was *essential* to the employer's business. Additionally the *Wards Cove* opinion held that the burden of persuasion remained with the employee throughout the proceedings, and, contrary to *Griggs,* did not shift to the employer upon a prima facie showing of disparate impact by the employee. The U.S. Supreme Court was sharply divided (five to four) in the *Wards Cove* case. Academics and congressional critics were divided regarding the case's impact.

Legislation restoring the burden on an employer to prove business necessity in disparate impact cases was enacted by Congress on November 13, 1991 and signed into law by President

Bush on November 21, 1991. That legislation, the Civil Rights Act of 1991, contains the specific findings in section 2 that:

(1) Additional remedies under Federal law are needed to deter unlawful harassment and intentional discrimination in the workplace;
(2) The decision of the Supreme Court in *Wards Cove Pack Co. v. Atonio,* 490 U.S. 642 (1989) has weakened the scope and effectiveness of Federal civil rights protection; and
(3) Legislation is necessary to provide additional protections against unlawful discrimination in employment.

Among the purposes of this new Act, as set forth in Section 3, is to codify the concepts of "business necessity" and "job related" ennunciated by the U.S. Supreme Court in the 1971 *Griggs* case and in other Supreme Court decisions prior to the 1989 *Wards Cove* case. Now, as a result, if an employee shows that an employment practice causes a disparate impact on the basis of race, color, religion, sex or national origin, the burden shifts to the employer under section 105(a) of the 1991 Act to demonstrate that the challenged practice is job related and consistent with business necessity. The burden of persuasion has now been returned to the employer on these issues, following the two and one-half year lapse resulting from the *Wards Cove* decision.

Undoubtedly, the application of these provisions will be the focus of debate in judicial and academic circles. For example, in signing the bill, President Bush stated that the Executive Branch will be guided by the remarks of Senator Dole and others introduced into the Congressional record on October 30 and November 5, 1991. In light of the return to the employer of the burden of persuasion of the business necessity defense, President Bush announced that, "it is especially important to insure that all the legislation's other safeguards against unfair application of disparate impact law are carefully observed," (Weekly Compilation of Presidential Documents, Monday, Nov. 25, 1991 at 1702). Section 105(b) of the Act, however, provides that only the interpretive memorandum appearing at volume 137 of the Congressional

Record at S15276 (daily ed. Oct. 25, 1991) shall be considered or relied on as legislative history in construing the Act.

A detailed examination of these differences in interpretation is outside the scope of this work, as is a discussion of other complexities in Title VII litigation. In the language-on-the-job context, however, several general principles remain clear. The EEOC and the courts have established the principle that discrimination based upon language can constitute unlawful national origin discrimination under Title VII. Accordingly, an employer who attempts to limit employment to those proficient in English or who speak the so-called "General American" accent (Van Riper in Matsuda, n. 121, p. 1361) runs a serious risk of liability under Title VII. That is because the cases discussed in this chapter, even where the plaintiffs ultimately lost, will make it fairly easy for workers harmed by such a blanket English proficiency requirement to at least make out a prima facie case of discrimination under Title VII. Once that has been established, if the case is brought as a disparate impact case, the burden now shifts to the employer to demonstrate the business necessity and job relatedness of the requirement. Even if the employer makes this showing, plaintiffs have an opportunity to rebut by demonstrating the feasibility of alternative employment practices which could have been utilized by the employer which would have had a lesser impact upon national origin minority workers. The Civil Rights Act of 1991, and previous law, provide the legal basis for such a showing. Plaintiffs will be able to demonstrate the increasing use in industry of models for accommodating limited English-speaking workers (see chapters 1 and 7 of this book). If the employer refuses to adopt such alternatives which would also serve the employer's legitimate interest in efficient and trustworthy workmanship, that fact will rebut the employers' claim that its language selection rule was used for non-discriminatory reasons (Rossein, pp. 2-53 and *Albermarle* case). Similarly, the increasing availability of such models of accommodation, especially at little or no cost to the employer, will make it more difficult for the employer facing a disparate treatment case to rebut a plaintiff's showing that the blanket proficiency requirement is only a pretext for intentional discrimination. Furthermore, the Civil Rights Act of 1991 has added the option of a jury trial. It has enhanced the remedies available, including the availability of punitive damages in intentional discrimination cases. The increasing risks and costs of Title VII litigation would seem to justify caution by management when considering a worker's language abilities in a hiring or promotion decision, particularly where the language ability standard actually exceeds what is needed for job-related communication.

42 U.S.C. §1981

Another federal statute, 42 U.S.C §1981, also potentially affords protection against language discrimination on the job. That statute, as originally enacted following the Civil War, provides:

> All persons within the jurisdiction of the United States shall have the same right in every state and territory to make and enforce contracts, to sue, be parties, give evidence, and to the full and equal benefit of all laws and proceedings for the security of persons and property as is enjoyed by white citizens.

Courts have interpreted this provision to protect against discriminatory hiring practices. Unlike the Equal Employment Opportunity Act cases, however, where a discrimination case can be made generally by showing disparate impact upon a protected group, courts have required that a discrimination claim under 42 U.S.C. §1981 provide proof of discriminatory intent. Thus, a Mr. Vasquez, who spoke only Spanish, had been periodically hired as a seasonal truck driver for the McAllen Bag and Supply Company in Texas and had performed his duties satisfactorily in the past, did not win his suit arising out of the refusal to rehire him after the company instituted a policy of hiring only English-speaking truck drivers. The Court found that while the policy would tend to discriminate against Mexican-Americans because a significant number do not speak English, it was not proven that an employer who could communicate with his drivers only in English had the requisite discriminatory motive in instituting a policy of hiring only English-speaking or bilingual truck drivers.

Although Mr. Vasquez did not succeed in his individual claim, his case and others like it recognize that Hispanics and other language minority peoples may be protected by section 1981. Although not in the employment context, the 1973 case of *Hernandez v. Erlenbusch* concluded that a tavern's rule prohibiting persons from speaking Spanish on the premises violated this provision.

42 U.S.C. 1981 has traditionally been interpreted to prohibit racial discrimination. In 1987 the U.S. Supreme Court broadened the definition of who would be protected by concluding that:

> Congress intended to protect from discrimination identifiable classes of persons who are subjected to intentional discrimination solely because of their ancestry or ethnic characteristics. Such discrimination is racial discrimination that Congress intended §1981 to forbid, whether or not it would be classified as racial in terms of modern scientific theory. (*St. Francis College* case, 481 U.S. at 613).

However, if the discrimination is based solely on national origin, 42 U.S.C. §1981 does not apply. Professor Rossein (1990) notes the difficulties in pleading and presenting a case involving potentially fine distinctions between these concepts in section 4.3(1) of his treatise. As is clear from these several cases, placing language concerns into these national origin or race pigeonholes is tricky.

Discrimination cases founded upon accent can also be brought under this section, although the willingness of courts to accept the defense of "inability to effectively communicate" would create the same hurdles for a plaintiff under this section as the "disparate treatment claim" of *Fragante.* Matsuda reports that in a 1981 case in the U.S. District Court for the Northern District of Illinois, a board-certified orthopedic surgeon was denied insurance in part because the insurer claimed his accent would make communication with patients and jurors difficult and therefore make him more susceptible to malpractice claims. He sued under section 1981, and lost. The Court, in page 3 of its opinion, stated:

Accent is relevant where, as here, the ability to communicate is at issue. There is no evidence that the ability to communicate effectively in English is not a reasonably necessary prerequisite either to a successful medical practice or to the ability to defend a lawsuit. Therefore, it was not unreasonable for the defendants to rely on the effect of Sirajullah's English language disability as one of the reasons for denying his application.

Another obstacle which temporarily faced section 1981 plaintiffs was the 1989 limitation of its application by the *Patterson* decision of the U.S. Supreme Court. There, the Court held that 42 U.S.C. §1981 does not apply to conditions of employment but only to discrimination in the formation of the employment contract or the right to enforce that contract. Language discrimination occurring after the hiring decision would not be actionable following *Patterson.* However, the Civil Rights Act of 1991 removed this obstacle. Section 101 of that Act amended 42 U.S.C. 1981 by defining "make and enforce contracts" to include the making, performance, modification and termination of contracts, and the enjoyment of all benefits, privileges, terms and conditions of the contractual relationship. Once again, 42 U.S.C. 1981 applies to language discrimination occurring not only at hiring, but also throughout the employment relationship.

If a person is able to overcome these obstacles and can prove that he or she was denied employment, promotions, or other employment benefits on the basis of unjustifiable language restrictions, that person would have a cause of action under both Title VII and 42 U.S.C. §1981. Among the major reasons why workers would choose to add a claim under 42 U.S.C. §1981 to a Title VII claim is that 42 U.S.C. §1981 does not have the procedurally complex time and waiting prerequisites imposed by Title VII. Professor Rossein's treatise should be consulted for a comprehensive discussion of the application of these and other antidiscrimination provisions.

Immigration Reform and Control Act of 1986 (IRCA)

As political pressures mounted to limit illegal immigration, congressional proposals were introduced to make illegal the hiring of unauthorized workers. The first "employer sanctions" bill was introduced in February 1952 but did not pass. Other proposals surfaced in 1971, and ultimately led to the enactment of the Immigration Reform and Control Act (IRCA) on November 6, 1986. The sanctions provision, section 101(a)(1), requires verification of work eligibility by employers and establishes penalties for employers who knowingly hire unauthorized aliens. The theory is that employment is the magnet attracting unauthorized aliens. Removing employment opportunities breaks the major "pull" factor.

Organized labor was among the leading proponents of employer sanctions. Among its leading opponents were agricultural growers, who were able to carve out a complex temporary worker program, and more favorable "amnesty" provisions than those provided to other aliens under IRCA.

A key controversy in the discussions leading to the passage of the sanction's provision was whether employers would begin to discriminate against foreign-looking or foreign-sounding citizens and legal aliens. As a result, the Act also prohibits employment discrimination on the basis of national origin and citizenship status. IRCA established a new enforcement unit within the Department of Justice known as the Office of the Special Counsel for Immigration-Related Unfair Employment Practices (OSC), which has the authority to prosecute complaints alleging national origin and citizenship status discrimination. Under the new antidiscrimination provisions, employers with four or more employees may not discriminate against any authorized worker in hiring, discharging, recruiting, or referring for a fee because of that individual's national origin or citizenship status. Employers who engage in unfair immigration-related discrimination may be ordered to hire, with or without back pay, individuals directly injured by the discrimination. They may also be required to pay a fine and keep certain records regarding the hiring of applicants and employees. Attorneys' fees may also be recovered by the prevailing party.

The interplay between the jurisdiction of the EEOC and the OSC is complex. There are cases where both agencies would have jurisdiction. IRCA, however, prohibits filing the same discrimination charges arising from the same set of facts with both agencies. A charging party is thus forced to file with one or the other. If the party makes the wrong choice, he or she may not be able to make a second filing with the other agency before the statute of limitations runs out. To prevent this from occurring, both agencies have referred charges to each other since the law passed.

An important concern, as noted, in enacting the IRCA, was the fear that its employer sanctions provisions would lead to unlawful national origin and citizenship discrimination. As a result, the Government Accounting Office (GAO) was instructed to determine whether a widespread pattern of discrimination resulted against eligible workers seeking employment solely from the implementation of the sanctions provision. Preparing its report, the GAO reviewed federal agency implementation of IRCA, reviewed discrimination complaints filed with federal agencies and data from groups representing the aliens, and used additional methods to obtain data on the IRCA's effects. These methodologies, according to the report, included a statistically valid survey of over 9,400 of the nation's employers, which projects to a universe of about 4.6 million employers. It also did a "hiring audit" in which pairs of persons matched closely on job qualifications applied for jobs with 360 employers in two cities. One member of each pair was a "foreign-appearing, foreign-sounding" Hispanic and the other was an Anglo with no foreign accent (GAO Report, p. 3). In sum, the General Accounting Office found that there was widespread discrimination, and that the discrimination was a direct result of the employer sanctions provisions of the IRCA. For example, 461,000 employers (or 10 percent of those surveyed) discriminated on the basis of a person's foreign appearance or accent–clearly national original discrimination. This is a conservative conclusion because the GAO assumed that nonrespondents did not discriminate even though it was likely that many of those who failed to respond were discriminating but would not admit it (p. 38). An estimated 227,000 employers (or 5 percent) reported that as a result of IRCA they began a practice not to hire persons because of foreign appearance or accent (p. 41). An estimated 346,000 employers (or 8 percent) reported that as a result of IRCA they applied the law's employment verification system only to foreign-looking or foreign-sounding persons. The GAO report concluded that the hiring audit shows a high level of national origin discrimination. To the extent that the sanctions provision results in new discrimination, it exacerbated an already serious problem of national origin employment discrimination (p. 49).

This report by the GAO is particularly troubling. Because the government had been unable to stop the flow of undocumented workers into this country, it chose to make private employers, in effect, private enforcers of the nation's immigration law. No compensation is paid to the private sector for this burden. IRCA and its underlying regulations are complex. Job applicants may present any of seventeen various documents to establish employment eligibility. On the basis of such documents, employers are required to complete an Employment Eligibility Verification Form (I–9) for each new employee. In making the certification on the I–9 that he or she has examined the documents, employers are expected to judge whether the documents presented are obviously fraudulent or counterfeit. If the employer violates the "sanctions" provision, criminal and civil penalties can be imposed. If he or she refuses to hire someone in violation of the prohibition of national origin discrimination, he or she can be liable for damages. The employer is placed between the proverbial rock and a hard place. The result, according to the GAO, is widespread discrimination. Potential employees who happen to look or sound *foreign* already facing *Fragante* type hiring decisions, now face a legislative scheme resulting in new discrimination. Congress can repeal the sanctions provisions; as of this writing, it has not done so.

The OSC has taken some steps to attempt to alleviate the discrimination. In newspaper advertisements it has attempted to inform employees that employment discrimination based upon language or foreign appearance is unlawful. In a typical advertisement appearing in the Sunday, May 19, 1991 edition of the *Lubbock Avalanche Journal* the OSC presents the reader with drawings of workers with the caption: "Not all these People were Born in America . . . But They're all Eligible to Work Here!" The text provides the following information:

Does the foreign-born appearance or ability to speak fluent English affect your decision about hiring a prospective employee?

The answer to this question must be "NO!" If you are confused about the new anti-discrimination laws, you should know the following:

Employers need not and must not discriminate against prospective employees who appear to be foreign-born.

After hiring, complete the Employment Eligibility Verification Form (I–9 Form). It accomplishes the task of verification of identity and employment authorization, simply and easily.

Don't let concerns about national origin, citizenship status or employment verification keep you from interviewing and hiring the best candidates. Hiring/firing/recruiting discrimination is against the law!

IF YOU HAVE QUESTIONS ABOUT COMPLETING FORM I–9 OR EMPLOYMENT DISCRIMINATION, CALL INS IN DALLAS AT (214)655-3078 OR THE OFFICE OF THE SPECIAL COUNSEL AT 1-800-255-7688

"YOU DON'T HAVE TO BE BORN IN AMERICA TO WORK IN AMERICA!"

The ad, which appeared nationwide, carries the seal of the U.S. Department of Justice. This author noticed similar ads in the New York City subway system in June 1991. Followup study is needed to determine their effectiveness. Some critics will undoubtedly argue the measure is too little, too late, given the documented widespread discrimination. Others might point out that the ad may go beyond the *Fragante* decision if the Justice Department takes the position that ability to speak fluent English must not affect an employer's decision about hiring a prospective employee. After all, courts upheld the employers' decisions in those cases where language ability (*Mejia*) and accent (*Fragante*) formed the basis of the employers' decision not to hire. Perhaps the OSC feels the protection afforded against national origin discrimination in IRCA should be broader than the similar prohibition under the EEOA. Or perhaps it feels the *Carino* type decisions reflect a better approach than the *Fragante* approach. Cases will have to be brought and make their way through the appellate courts before we can gain further judicial insight into how such matters will be resolved in the adversary (litigation) system. Chapter 6 of this book suggests a comprehensive legal analysis that focuses on the real issues at stake, and Chapter 7 set forth what may be more efficient models for resolution.

Proficiency in Language Other Than English

Thus far this chapter has been concerned with a discussion of the right of an employer to limit employment to those people who speak only English and those who speak English with no accent. Given the recent dramatic increase in the Spanish-speaking population, however, would an employer be justified in imposing a requirement that his or her employees demonstrate proficiency in Spanish or some other foreign language? The answer appears to be that if language proficiency can be shown to be supported by a business necessity (such as being able to serve as an interpreter or responding to the requests of customers in another language) the imposition of foreign language proficiency would be upheld. The U.S. Border Patrol, for example, requires that its officers be proficient in Spanish. On the other hand, if foreign language proficiency is used to exclude other racial or national origin groups without a showing of a business necessity, the imposition would probably constitute impermissible discrimination. In the immigration law context, an employer seeking to bring in a foreign worker as a permanent resident of this country cannot include a foreign language requirement in the job description which the U.S. Department of Labor must approve, unless adequately documented as arising from business necessity (20 C.F.R §656.21(b)(2)).

It will be interesting to note if monolingual, English-speaking Americans suddenly become sensitized to language rights issues if they find themselves denied employment opportunities because of a language barrier. In one recent case, a court upheld the validity of an employer's hiring requirement that employees be bilingual, given the large Spanish-speaking clientele. Professor David Gregory finds it quite possible that some employers in Miami, for example, where more than 55 percent of the population is Hispanic might legitimately require all employees to speak Spanish to Spanish-speaking customers or to have bilingual capability. Professor Player, on the other hand, believes that while an English-speaking employer could deny employment to non-English speaking applicants on the grounds they could not communicate with him, he infers that a non-English-speaking employer would be required to hire an interpreter rather than deny employment to monolingual English-speakers (Player, p. 236). The Player approach appears inconsistent. Comprehensive approaches to these and other job-related language issues are set forth in the reexamination sections in Chapter 6 and the accommodation models described in Chapter 7. Those approaches will be more understandable after we finish the applications and critiques in the chapters to follow.

Bibliography

Books

1. Frank Bean, Georges Vernez, Charles B. Keely, *Opening and Closing Doors: Evaluating Immigration Reform and Control* (1989).

2. Bill Piatt, *Only English? Law & Language Policy in the United States* (1990).

3. Mack A. Player, *Employment Discrimination Law* (1988).

4. Merrick T. Rossein, *Employment Discrimination Law and Litigation* (1990).

Articles

1. John W. Aniol, Note, *Language Discrimination Under Title VII: The Silent Right of National Origin Discrimination,* 15 J. Marshall L. Rev. 667 (1982).

2. David L. Gregory, *Union Leadership and Workers' Voices: Meeting the Needs of Linguistically Heterogeneous Union Members,* 58 Cinc. L. Rev. 115 (1989).

3. Mari J. Matsuda, *Voices of America: Accent, Antidiscrimination Law and a Jurisprudence for the Last Reconstruction,* 100 Yale L.J. 1329 (1991).

4. Van Riper, *General American: An Ambiguity,* in Harold B. Allen & Michael D. Linn, eds., Dialect and Language Variation (1986).

Selected Judicial and Administrative Decisions

1. *Albermarle Paper Co. v. Moody*, 422 U.S. 405 (1975).

2. *Bell v. Home Life Ins. Co.,* 596 F. Supp. 1549 (M.D.N.C. 1984).

3. *Berke v. Ohio Dept. of Public Welfare*, 628 F.2d 980 (6th Cir. 1980).

4. *Carino v. Univ. of Oklahoma Bd. of Regents*, 750 F.2d 815 (10th Cir. 1984).

5. Case No. YAU 9-048, 2 Fair Empl. Prac. Cas. (BNA) 78 (EEOC 1969).

6. *Espinoza v. Farah Mfg. Co.*, 414 U.S. 86 (1973).

7. *Fragante v. City and County of Honolulu*, 699 F.Supp. 1429 (D. Hawaii 1987), 888 F.2d 591 (9th Cir. 1989).

8. *Griggs v. Duke Power Co.*, 401 U.S. 424 (1971), (disparate impact guidelines under Title VII).

9. *Hernandez v. Erlenbusch*, 368 F. Supp. 752 (D.C. Or. 1973).

10. *Hou v. Pennsylvania*, 573 F.Supp. 1539 (W.D. Pa. 1983).

11. *Jones v. United Gas Improvement Corp.*, 68 F.R.D. 1 (E.D. Pa. 1975).

12. *Kahakua v. Hallgrem*, No. 86-0434 (D. Hawaii 1987), *aff'd sub nom, Kahakua v. Friday*, 876 F.2d 896 (9th Cir. 1989) (text in Westlaw).

13. *Local 189, United Papermakers and Paperworkers v. United States*, 416 F.2d 980 (5th Cir. 1969), cert. denied, 397 U.S. 919 (1970) (employer not required to train unqualified employees).

14. *Louiseau v. Dept. of Human Resources of Or.*, 567 F. Supp. 1211 (D.Or. 1983).

15. *McDonnel Douglas Corp. v. Green*, 411 U.S. 792 (1973) (disparate treatment guidelines under Title VII).

16. *Mejia v. New York Sheraton Hotel*, 459 F. Supp. 375 (S.D.N.Y. 1978).

17. *Patterson v. McClean Credit Union*, 491 U.S. 164 (1989).

18. *Perez v. F.B.I.*, 707 F.Supp. 891, 714 F. Supp. 1414 (W.D.Tex. 1989).

19. *St. Francis College v. Al-Khazraii*, 481 U.S. 604, *reh'g denied* 483 U.S.1011 (1987).

20. *Sirajullah v. Illinois State Medical Inter-Ins. Exch.*, No. 86-C–
    8868 (N.D. Ill. 1989).
21. *Smith v. D.C.*, 29 Fair Empl. Prac. Cas. (BNA) 1129 (D.C. Cir.
    1982) (bilingual job requirement upheld).

22. *Vasquez v. McAllen Bag & Supply Co.*, 660 F.2d 686 (5th Cir.
    1981), *cert. denied,* 458 U.S. 1122 (1982).

23. *Wards Cove Packing Co. v. Atonio*, 490 U.S. 642 (1989).

24. *Yu Cong Eng v. Trinidad*, 271 U.S. 500 (1926) (Due process right
    of non-English speaking merchant to keep records in an under
    standable language).

Federal Statutes, Regulations

1. 20 C.F.R. §656.21(b)(2) (1991) (Basic Labor Certification Process).

2. 29 C.F.R. §1606.1 (1971 and 1980) (Definition of National Origin
   Discrimination).

3. 29 C.F.R. §1606.7 (1991) (Speak English-Only Rules)

4. Civil Rights Act of 1866, ch. 31, §1, 14 Stat. 27, current version at
   42 U.S.C. §1981 (1982).

5. Civil Rights Act of 1991, Pub. L. No. 102-166, 105 Stat. 1071.

6. Immigration Reform & Control Act of 1986, (Pub. L. No. 99-603,
   100 Stat. 3359) (codified as amended in scattered sections of 7
   U.S.C., 8 U.S.C., 18 U.S.C., 20 U.S.C., 29 U.S.C., & 42 U.S.C.)
   (1986); Pub. L. No. 100-203, 101 Stat. 1330 (current version at 42
   U.S.C. §673)(1987).

7. Title VII, Civil Rights Act of 1964, Pub. L. No. 88-352, Title VII,
   78 Stat. 253, 42 U.S.C. §2000e-2000e-17 1982 & Supp. V 1987).

Other Materials

1. U.S. Govt. Accounting Office Report to the Congress, *Immigration Reform: Employer Sanctions and the Question of Discrimination* GAO/66D-90-62, March 1990.

2. 137 Cong. Rec. S15276 (daily ed. Oct. 25, 1991), 137 Cong. Rec. S15472-S15478 (daily ed. Oct. 30, 1991), and 137 Cong. Rec. S15953 (daily ed. Nov. 5, 1991) (regarding Civil Rights Act of 1991).

3. 27 WEEKLY COMP. PRES. DOC. 1699-1702 (Nov. 25, 1991).

CHAPTER THREE

Communication Among Employees

Suppose that a multilingual applicant has been hired. Does the employer have the right to prohibit the employee from using languages other than English on the job? As noted in Chapter 1, historically employers were generally accommodating, in need of immigrant laborers, and did not resort to the use of "speak-English only" rules. Where such rules were in effect they apparently were not the subject of legal challenges. Such rules, in any event, would obviously be meaningless where the work force either speaks only English or speaks only a foreign tongue. However, the rise in bilingualism in this country, particularly involving the Spanish language, and a resultant nativist attempt to limit the use of languages other than English, have produced recent legal developments impacting the work place.

In this chapter we will consider those developments and attempt to determine under what circumstances, if any, employers may lawfully restrict the language usage of their employees.

Early Challenges

The reported history of challenges to speak English only rules is relatively short, coinciding with the application of the Equal Employment Opportunity Act (see Chapter 2) to them. A 1970 decision of the EEOC made it clear that an absolute prohibition against foreign language communication among employees constitutes national origin discrimination by the employer. In that case, the rule prohibited the use of Spanish on the work premises, and the employer offered no evidence of any business necessity for the rule. Three years later the EEOC found it unlawful for an employer and a labor union at a food processing company to prohibit employees from speaking Spanish during work hours and at union meetings.

In 1979, in a case decided by the U.S. District Court for the Southern District of Texas, the application of a broad English only rule was held unlawful. In that case, a Mexican American employee was discharged for speaking two words of Spanish on the job. Another employee of the same firm was retained even though the second employee was guilty of the more serious misdeed of engaging in a fight during the same incident. The business in that case involved the drilling of a well. The Court found that while the operation of a drilling rig is a highly skilled, dangerous operation requiring close coordination between members of the crew, and while ordinarily some limitation on the use of language other than English might be appropriate for the business necessity of the safety of personnel and protection of property, the utterance of a casual phrase that caused no failure in communication and no danger could not form the basis of a discharge of the employee.

However, a similar utterance was held to be lawfully within the prohibition imposed by a speak English only rule in a decision concerning a Mr. Garcia, who worked as a salesman in a lumber store in Brownsville, Texas. More than three-fourths of the population in the business area was Hispanic, and many of the store's customers expressed the desire to be waited on by Spanish-speaking sales people. Garcia was hired precisely because he was bilingual and was able to accommodate customers. He was instructed to use English with English speaking customers and Spanish with Spanish speaking customers. However, the owner imposed another language rule on Garcia: even though three-fourths of the store's workers and customers spoke Spanish, Garcia and all other Spanish-speaking employees were forbidden from speaking Spanish on the job unless communicating with a Spanish-speaking customer. Among the reasons given by the owner for this rule was that the English-speaking customers (only one-fourth of the total population in the area) objected to the

Spanish-speaking employees communicating among themselves in a language that the monolingual English customers did not understand. One day Garcia was asked a question by another Spanish-speaking clerk about an item requested by a customer. Garcia responded to the co-worker in Spanish that the article was not available. The owner overheard this exchange and fired Garcia. In rejecting Garcia's claim for relief under Title VII, the District Court found there were valid business reasons for the rule. On appeal, the Fifth Circuit Court upheld the District Court, refusing to critically examine either the validity of the business reasons offered or whether the business needs could be met in a less restrictive manner than by the imposition of an English only rule. The Court found Garcia's conduct to be a deliberate violation of the rule, concluding that the language that a bilingual person elects to speak at a particular time is a matter of choice.

In 1981, a year after the Garcia case, another court upheld an English only rule. In the case of *Flores v. Hartford Police Department*, the U. S. District Court for the District of Connecticut held that the "absolute-no-Spanish rule" at a police academy did not violate Title VII. In the same year, the EEOC struck down an English-only rule for tailor shop employees, finding it was not justified simply because fellow employees and customers preferred the "speak-English-only rule." However, two years later, in 1983, the EEOC held that an English-only rule in a petroleum refinery laboratory was justified by the necessity of safe and efficient operations, where employees were required to work with potentially dangerous chemicals in a laboratory setting.

In 1987, the Ninth Circuit Court of Appeals upheld the termination of a radio disk jockey who claimed that the employer's English-only rule violated Title VII. The employer had fired the announcer for speaking Spanish on the air in violation of the English-only broadcasting rule. In that case, the Court concluded there was a valid business necessity for the rule: a programming decision motivated by marketing, ratings, and demographic concerns.

Contemporary View: EEOC Guidelines and Gutierrez

The *Garcia* decision, although upholding a speak-English rule, made clear that its holding was limited to actual on the job language usage and would not extend to lunch hours and work breaks. The Fifth Circuit also noted, in reaching its decision, that no EEOC guideline applied to such cases. It implied (at Note 1 on page 268 of its decision), that it would have deferred to such guidelines if any had existed.

Soon after the Garcia decision was announced, in 1980, the EEOC did issue such guidelines. The commission announced its concern that employees should be protected from discriminatory employment practices and unnecessary barriers, such as arbitrary English-only work rules. These 1980 regulations were incorporated into a set of guidelines issued by the EEOC in 1987. These guidelines, set forth at 29 C.F.R. Section 1606.7, create a presumption that rules requiring employees to speak English at all times in the work place violate Title VII as national origin discrimination. In this regard, the rule states:

> A rule requiring employees to speak only English at all times in the work place is a burdensome term and condition of employment. The primary language of an individual is often an essential national origin characteristic. Prohibiting employees at all times, in the work place, from speaking their primary language or the language they speak comfortably, disadvantages an individual's employment opportunities on the basis of national origin. It may also create an atmosphere of inferiority, isolation and intimidation based on national origin which could result in a discriminatory working environment. Therefore, the Commission will presume that such a rule violates Title VII and will closely scrutinize it.

However, the EEOC guideline leaves open the possibility that in some limited circumstances, an employer could create a limited language rule:

> An employer may have a rule requiring that employees speak only
> English at certain times where the employer can show that the rule is
> justified by business necessity.

In 1986, this author published an article in the *Houston Law Review* criticizing the *Garcia* rationale, and urging broader recognition of language rights in the work place. In 1988, the principles embodied in the EEOC regulation, this author's *Houston Law Review* article, and other sources were applied by the Ninth Circuit Court of Appeals in a case that expanded the right of a worker to speak a language other than English on the job (*Gutierrez v. Municipal Court*). An examination of this case is important because it will likely continue to serve as persuasive authority in future language rights cases stemming from speak-English rules at work.

Alva Gutierrez, and a number of other bilingual Hispanics were employed as deputy court clerks by the Southeast Judicial District of the Los Angeles Municipal Court. In March 1984 the Municipal Court, through its judges, enacted a new rule forbidding employees to speak any language other than English, except when acting as translators. The rule read:

> The English language shall be spoken by all court employees during
> regular working hours while attending to assigned work duties, unless
> an employee is translating for the non-English speaking public. This
> rule does not apply to employees while on their lunch hour or work
> breaks.

Ms. Gutierrez challenged the rule under Title VII using both disparate impact and disparate treatment theories. She also brought suit against the judges based on another post-Civil War Civil Rights Statute, 42 U.S.C. Section 1983. (The Act prohibits persons, acting under color of state law, from violating the federally protected civil rights of another.) She contended that the rule, although allegedly neutral, nonetheless unfairly disadvantaged Hispanics because their ethnic identity is linked to the use of the Spanish language. She argued alternatively that the rule was intentionally adopted for the purpose of discriminating against Hispanics. She thus claimed that any neutral appearance was a mere pretext and violated the Title VII proscriptions against disparate treatment as well as creating a disparate impact upon a protected national origin group.

In upholding an injunction against the rule, the Ninth Circuit Court of Appeals, citing sources including this author, found that the multicultural character of American society has a long and venerable history and is widely recognized as one of the United States' greatest strengths. It noted that while few courts have evaluated the lawfulness of work place rules relating to the use of languages other than English, commentators generally agree that language is an important aspect of national origin. It noted with approval this author's conclusion that the primary language of an individual not only conveys certain concepts but is itself an affirmation of that person's culture. It distinguished the case from issues in the *Jurado* ruling, noting that while an employer has a right to insist that a broadcast be conducted exclusively in English because that is the product the employer was offering the public, the *Jurado* case did not involve an employer who was requiring employees to conduct off-the-air conversations in English. The Court adopted with approval the EEOC guidelines.

The appeals court had little difficulty disposing of the justifications offered by the municipal court judges for their English-only rule, and the reasoning applied will undoubtedly shape the course of future case decisions in this area. First, the employer asserted that because the United States is an English-speaking country, and California is an English-speaking state (as evidenced by its 1986 constitutional amendment making English the official language of the state), the Municipal Court would be justified in imposing English-only rules on its employees. The Ninth Circuit found this reason without merit. It noted that the prohibition of intra-employee Spanish communication does little to achieve English-speaking country and state status given that as part of their official duties, the Court's bilingual employees are required to communicate in Spanish on a regular basis with numerous members of the non-English speaking public. Next, the employers argued that the rule would be necessary to prevent the work place from turning into a Tower of Babel. The Court concluded that allowing Spanish to be spoken is unlikely to create a much greater disruption than already exists, given that speaking in Spanish is necessary to the normal conduct of court business. Third, the employer argued the rule is necessary to promote racial harmony. The Court found this argument to be "generally unpersuasive," again citing this author and noting that racial hostility *increased* among Hispanics and non-Spanish speaking employees because Hispanics felt belittled by the English-only regulation. When the Court considered the fourth argument of employers, that the English-only rule was necessary because several supervisors did not speak Spanish, the Court concluded that the best way to ensure supervisors are apprised of how well the bilingual employees are performing their task would be to employ Spanish-speaking supervisors. Finally, the Court concluded that the California "official English" constitutional amendment does not create a business necessity. (More on the role of state legislative attempts to bootstrap a business necessity follows in the next section.)

The *Gutierrez* opinion was issued by a three-judge panel of the Ninth Circuit. The municipal court judges, who were the employers losing the *Gutierrez* case, sought to have the entire Ninth Circuit rehear the case. Their request was denied, with one judge dissenting. They then sought review by the U. S. Supreme Court. In a one-paragraph opinion, the Supreme Court found the case moot. Although the summary opinion does not identify why the Court found the case to be moot, counsel for the municipal judges had urged in his briefs that the "English only" rule had never gone into effect, and that in any event it could not be applied to Ms. Gutierrez because she no longer worked for the Municipal Court. He also urged that a monetary settlement paid by the county of Los Angeles to Ms. Gutierrez made her case moot. Any or all of these reasons could have formed the basis for the Supreme Court ruling. Counsel for the defendant municipal judges, in a phone conversation with this author, stated he was never informed as to which of these reasons became the basis for the "mootness" decision. In May 1989 the Ninth Circuit, upon order by the Supreme Court, vacated its opinion and dismissed the appeal. Nonetheless, the reasoning in the *Gutierrez* opinion of the Ninth Circuit's three-judge panel is still persuasive for other language rights cases which will undoubtedly follow. For example, in July 1989, a U. S. District Court in California enjoined the City of Pomona, California, from enforcing an ordinance requiring businesses with signs using foreign alphabetical characters to devote 50 percent of the sign space to English. The Court favorably cited *Gutierrez* for the proposition that discrimination based on language constitutes discrimination based on national origin. The Court in that case relied upon the First Amendment to the United States Constitution (freedom of expression) in prohibiting the application of the ordinance.

The confusion created in the wake of the *Wards Cove* case (see Chapter 2) regarding the temporary dilution of the employer's business necessity burden caused much commentary. One particularly well reasoned analysis involving language issues (Mealey in the 1989 *Minnesota Law Review*), concluded that courts should follow the EEOC guidelines that equate language with national origin. She argues that courts should now recognize a rebuttable presumption that English-only rules have a disparate impact on national origin. She also concludes that courts should find that such rules create a burden on members of national origin groups, even those who are bilingual, because they still bear a higher risk of incurring penalties than do employees who speak English as their primary language. She urges that courts preclude the unjustified use of seemingly facially neutral language restrictions that impose burdensome conditions of employment on national origin groups. Her approach rings all the more true, now that Congress has returned the burden of proving the business necessity and job relatedness of such rules to employers.

Will State Official-English Laws Justify or Even Require English-Only Work Rules?

Our examination of the validity of speak-English-only work place rules would not be complete without some consideration of attempts to make English the official language of the states and the nation. These laws have been offered as justification for language-restrictive work rules, and the English-only movement continues to advocate such proscriptions. A brief digression is important. These eighteen states now have some form of official English laws on their books: Alabama, Arizona, Arkansas, California, Colorado, Florida, Georgia, Hawaii, Illinois, Indiana, Kentucky, Mississippi, Nebraska, North Carolina, North Dakota, South Carolina, Tennessee, and Virginia. Most of these acts are the recent result of the "English only" and "English first" movement. They appear to be part of a well orchestrated and well financed move to eventually attempt to persuade the United States Congress and the states to adopt a national constitutional amendment. That amendment, if adopted, would break with our tradition of promoting national unity by inclusion of diverse peoples, languages, and cultures. For the first time in our history, it would declare a language to be "official." (An analysis and critique of this approach is discussed at length in this author's 1990 book *¿Only English? Law and Language Policy in the United States.*) However, merely adding up a list of eighteen states does not give a complete picture. Georgia's resolution was not signed by its governor. Hawaii declares English to be official but also makes Hawaiian official. The application of California's constitutional amendment was limited in the *Gutierrez* case. Arizona's constitutional amendment was held unconstitutional (see below). Several states, including New Mexico and Louisiana, officially and explicitly recognize the importance of Spanish and French respectively. English-only legislative initiatives have recently been rejected in a number of states including Kansas, Louisiana, New Mexico, Oklahoma, Wyoming, Oregon, and Texas. Further details regarding state legislative enactments and how those interplay with other state and federal statutes, case decisions, administrative regulations, and constitutional provisions can be found in this author's works cited in the bibliography. Other materials in the bibliography offer further insight. For purposes of this chapter, however, it is important to determine whether these acts will justify or require English-only work place rules. Based on the cases so far, the answer is "no." Well intentioned employers should not be misled into thinking such acts require restrictive language rules; not-so-well-intentioned employers should not attempt to use them as a justification because courts will find such attempts ineffective, at least, or a pretext for purposeful unlawful discrimination at worst.

We have already considered one of these cases—*Gutierrez*. The employer there raised as a justification that California's official-English amendment created a business necessity for the English-only work rule. California's amendment (Article III, section 6) on its face seemed to offer some support for the employer's approach. The amendment reads in part:

a. Purpose

English is the common language of the people of the United States of America and the State of California. This section is intended to preserve, protect and strengthen the English language, and not to supersede any of the rights guaranteed to the people by this constitution.

b. English is the official language of the state of California.

c. Enforcement

The Legislature shall enforce this section by appropriate legislation. The Legislature and *officials of the state of California shall take all steps necessary to insure that the role of English as the common language of the state of California is preserved and enhanced* (emphasis added).

In rejecting the argument by the employer that the amendment required the use of English in all official state business and thus requires Hispanic employees to communicate in English while at work, the Court noted that the provision appeared to be "primarily a symbolic statement concerning the importance of preserving, protecting and strengthening the English language." It did not require imposition of an English-only work rule. Also, the Court noted that the adoption of a constitutional provision or a state statute does not by that fact create a business necessity. It cited the 1977 *Dothard* decision of the U.S. Supreme Court for that proposition. In *Dothard* the Court prohibited the application of Alabama's facially neutral statute specifying minimum height and weight requirements of five feet two inches and 120 pounds for employment as a prison guard, because the impact of that statute was to preclude many women from employment in violation of Title VII. The Ninth Circuit noted that a state enactment cannot constitute a business justification for the adoption of a discriminatory rule unless the state measure itself meets the business necessity test; otherwise, employers would be able to justify discriminatory regulations by relying on state laws that encourage or require discriminatory conduct. The Court noted that for federal law purposes, such as application of Title VII or 42 U.S.C. 1981, it would be immaterial whether inadequate justifications directly underlie the actions of a government agency or are incorporated in the constitution of a state. The Court noted that in either case if the preferred justifications failed to meet the business necessity test, they are legally insufficient. Accordingly, the constitutional provision could not serve as a justification for the municipal courts rule.

Another case, *Yniquez v. Mofford*, considered the constitutionality of the 1988 amendment to the Arizona state constitution, Article XXVIII, which declared English to be the official language of that state. This provision contained language comparable to the California amendment requiring that the state and its political subdivisions "take all reasonable steps to preserve, protect and enhance the role of the English language as the official language." But it went farther. With only a few exceptions, the article provided that all government entities and employees were prohibited from using any language other than English during the performance of government business.

The constitutionality of this amendment was raised in a lawsuit brought by a state employee. Until enactment of the Arizona amendment, the employee, an insurance claims adjuster, often spoke Spanish with Spanish-speaking persons who were bringing medical malpractice claims against the state. The Court found that the provision was unlawfully overbroad and unconstitutionally vague. The plain language of the amendment demonstrated that it was essentially a blanket prohibition against the use of non-English languages by any government employee during the performance of government business.

In both of these cases, courts determined that the existence of state "official English" and "English-only" provisions did not justify state employers restricting the language usage of its employees. While no case has appeared where a private employer attempted to offer an English-only statute or constitutional amendment as a justification for a work place language restriction rule, it would appear even less likely that a court would uphold such a justification. After all, if a state law cannot be used as justification for imposing English-only work rules upon state employees, it seems even more remote that such a restriction could serve as an adequate justification for such a rule by private employers. New "official-English" laws are likely to be treated only as symbolic expressions of pride in the English language if they are written loosely (*Gutierrez*) or as constitutionally defective if they are tightly written to prohibit the use of other tongues (*Yniquez*).

Nonetheless, the existence of these acts has led to some attempts to impose English-only work rules. As noted by the *New York Times* in an article on August 8, 1990, a Coral Gables grocery store manager suspended a cashier for speaking Spanish on the job immediately after Florida enacted its constitutional amendment making English the official state language in November 1988. After the case received publicity, the grocery chain issued a quick apology and transferred the manager.

The Future?

Attorneys for the EEOC and other civil rights attorneys indicate an increasing number of language restrictions at the work place. Some of them can be resolved outside of the courts, and Chapter 6 of this book offers some guidelines for such resolution. Others can be resolved by contact with an employer by the employee's attorney. In 1987 the Salvation Army removed speak-English-only rules from its employee handbooks after a complaint by a Latina employee. In 1988 the University of California at San Francisco Medical Center repealed its English-only policy after intervention by the EEOC (*Los Angeles Times,* Oct. 26, 1991). A life insurance company in Los Angeles in 1989 agreed to rescind its English-only policy after a complaint from the attorney representing a Chinese-speaking worker (*New York Times,* Aug. 8, 1990). Other cases will apparently require judicial examination. For example, the EEOC is pursuing a case involving a Hispanic clerk-typist at a Sears Roebuck and Company billing office in Los Angeles who has sued Sears over a rule forbidding her to speak Spanish at work.

At least two other cases are currently being pursued which could eventually give the U.S. Ninth Circuit Court of Appeals another opportunity to consider the validity of restrictive speak-English-only rules. The Ninth Circuit could reinstate the *Gutierrez* principles, giving them mandatory effect which is now only persuasive due to the mootness decision of the United States Supreme Court. Or, the court could limit *Gutierrez.* Accordingly, these cases will be important ones to follow through the appellate process.

The first of these cases, *Dimaranan v. Pomona Valley Hospital* went to trial before a U.S. District Court in California in April 1991. In that case, Ms. Adelaida Dimaranan, a Filipina nurse, sued her employer. She contended that the hospital's policy which precluded her from using Tagalog, her native language, violated her civil rights. On October 21, 1991 Judge Edward Rafeedie ruled that while the language policy was not motivated by ethnic animosity, the hospital had unlawfully retaliated against Ms. Dimaranan by demoting her from her position as assistant head of the mother-baby ward after she complained about the rule. The court concluded that the rule, which Ms. Dimaranan contended applied even during breaks, was promulgated because of concern over the breakdown of cohesion between Filipino and non-Filipino nurses and not because of concern over use of language. Her opposition to the rule, which she reasonably believed to be unlawful, was protected, the Court determined. The hospital was ordered to transfer Ms. Dimaranan to a position comparable to her previous one and to eliminate negative evaluations from her file. She was also awarded back pay. The hospital announced it intended to appeal the portion of the decision regarding back pay. The plaintiff's attorneys were considering appealing the judge's ruling to the Ninth Circuit as of this writing (December 1991), fearing that the ruling could encourage other employers to adopt similar language restrictions. Tension between employees arising from the use of a "foreign" language on the job, the reader may recall, was held insufficient justification in the *Gutierrez* case for a speak-English-only rule.

Another case which may result in a Ninth Circuit review of these issues is *Garcia v. Spun Steak Company.* On October 4, 1991 Judge Robert Schnacke, a U.S. District Court judge in California issued a permanent injunction against the English-only rule of a San Francisco meat packing plant. Up to sixty percent of the employees speak English, and English fluency was not required at hiring. The company defended its rule as necessary to avoid friction among employees, and to improve safety and productivity. In enjoining the rule, Judge Schnacke found that less restrictive alternatives can be used for discipline matters, and that production quotas could be used to increase productivity, rather than imposing a ban on the use of languages. He noted that the 1986 California constitutional amendment at issue in *Guttierrez* had emboldened employers improperly to enact such unlawful speak-English-only rules. Notice of appeal of this decision was filed on October 30, 1991. There are obvious inconsistencies between this opinion issued by Judge Schnacke and the Northern District of the U.S. District Court in California and that of Judge Rafeedie in the *Dimaranan* case, decided in the Central District of the U.S. District Court in California. Either or both of these cases, or the very likely prospect of increasingly inconsistent further decisions, might make ultimate considerations by the Ninth Circuit necessary.

Other cases are arising as well. In a phone conversation with this author, an EEOC attorney in California, Dolores Luciano noted that several were winding their way through the administrative process as of May 1991. A spokeswoman for the Mexican-American Legal Defense and Educational Fund, Martha Jimenez, cited in the *New York Times* article, indicated that her office was involved in at least eight language discrimination cases and was assigning a lawyer to work on that topic full-time. She, and other civil rights attorneys, indicated that the adoption of English-language statutes in many states in recent years was causing the spread of restrictive language usage rules in the work place.

There is probably no way to determine the number or extent of speak-English-only rules. The EEOC guidelines, the cases, and other authorities suggest that an employer's limitation on the right of a worker to speak to a co-worker in the co-worker's language of choice will be upheld, if challenged, in only limited circumstances. Thus, while nativist fears of the presence of multilingual workers speaking languages not understood by everyone may provoke fears and result in the creation of stringent speak-English-only rules, the courts, when called upon, will undoubtedly continue to serve as a strong limiting factor.

Another force may eventually also be at least as effective as the courts in limiting the application of speak-English-only rules. The marketplace, with its increasing numbers of language minority workers and consumers, might create a flexibility among otherwise unenlightened employers and courts. Professor David L. Gregory's 1988 study concludes these factors will play an important role in limiting the application of future English-only rules in the work place:

> Given the labor shortage already severely afflicting some employers, and projected to become more exacerbated in the coming decade, pristine niceties of case law may soon become quite academic. Rather than seek to refine rigid "English-only" work rules ad infinitum, even the most parochial employers may be pragmatically forced by changing work force demographics to not only tolerate, but affirmatively to seek out multi-lingual and multi-cultural employees in order to staff operations with sufficient personnel. Fortunately, the "English-only" work rule cases are now destined for quick obsolescence by labor shortages and rapidly changing work place demographics, and need not await the evolution of a more sensitive jurisprudence." (p. 126)

Bibliography

Articles

1. Michele Arington, Note, *English-Only Laws and Direct Legislation: The Battle in the States over Language Minority Rights,* 7 Journal of Law & Politics 325 (1991).

2. Irene Chang, *Ruling On Foreign Language Ban Criticized,* L.A. Times, Oct. 26, 1991, Metro, at B3.

3. David L. Gregory, *Union Leadership and Workers' Voices: Meeting the Needs of Linguistically Heterogeneous Union Members,* 58 Cinc. L. Rev. 115 (1989).

4. Linda M. Mealey, Note, *English-Only Rules and "Innocent" Employers: Clarifying National Origin Discrimination and Disparate Impact Theory under Title VII,* 74 Minn. L. Rev. 387 (1989).

5. Seth Mydans, *Pressure for English-Only Job Rules Stirring Sharp Debate Across U.S.,* N.Y. Times, Aug. 8, 1990 at A12.

6. Juan F. Perea, *English-Only Rules and the Right to Speak One's Primary Language in the Workplace,* 23 Journal of Law Reform 265 (1990).

7. Bill Piatt, *Toward Domestic Recognition of a Human Right to Language,* 23 Hous. L. Rev. 885 (1986).

8. Note, *"Official English": Federal Limits on Efforts to Curtail Bilingual Services in the States,* 100 Harv. L. Rev. 1345 (1987).

Selected Judicial and Administrative Decisions

1. *Asian American Business Group v. City of Pomona,* 716 F. Supp. 1328 (C.D. Cal. 1989).

2 .Commission Decision No. 71-446, 2 Fair Empl. Prac. Cas. (BNA) 1127 (EEOC 1970).

3. Commission Decision 73-0479, 19 Fair Empl. Prac. Cas. (BNA) 11788 (EEOC 1973).

4. Commission Decision 81-25, 27 Fair Empl. Prac. Cas. (BNA) 1820 (EEOC 1981).

5. Commission Decision No. 83-7, 31 Fair Empl. Prac. Cas. (BNA) 1861 (EEOC 1983).

6. *Dimaranan v. Pomona Valley Hospital,* No. CV 89-4299-EN (C.D. Cal.); 60 U.S.L.W. 2359 (Dec. 3, 1991).

7. *Dothard v. Rawlinson,* 433 U.S. 321 (1977).

8. *Flores v. Hartford Police Dept.,* 25 Fair Empl. Prac. Cas. (BNA) 180 (D. Conn. 1981).

9. *Garcia v. Gloor,* 618 F.2d 264, (5th Cir. 1980), *cert. denied,* 449 U.S. 1113 (1981).

10. *Garcia v. Spun Steak Co.,* No. C91-1949 RHS (N.D. Cal.), Daily Labor Report (BNA) No. 196, Oct. 9, 1991, A8, 1991 WL 268021.

11. *Gutierrez v. Mun. Ct. of S.E. Judicial Dist.,* 838 F.2d 1031 (9th Cir. 1988), *vacated as moot,* 109 S.Ct. 1736 (1989).

12. *Jurado v. Eleven-Fifty Corp.,* 813 F.2d 1406 (9th Cir. 1987).

13. *Saucedo v. Brothers Well Service, Inc.,* 464 F. Supp. 919 (S.D. Tex. 1979).

14. *Wards Cove Packing Co* v. Atonio, 490 U.S. 642 (1989

15. *Yniquez v. Mofford,* 730 F. Supp. 309 (D. Ariz. 1990).

Federal Statutes and Regulations

1. 29 C.F.R. section 1606.7 (1988) ("Speak-English-Only" rules).

2. Act of April 20, 1871, ch. 22, section 1, 17 Stat. 13 (current version at 42 U.S.C. section 1983 (1981)).

CHAPTER FOUR

COMMUNICATION BETWEEN EMPLOYEES AND CUSTOMERS

Suppose that a multilingual employee has satisfied the linguistic proficiency requirements of an employer (see Chapter 2) and is either not subject to, or is not quarreling with, a speak-English-only rule (scc Chapter 3). In fact, assume that the employer is quite enthused with the multilingual abilities of the employee and indeed requires the employee to use these skills on the job in communicating with potential customers to further the business interests of the employer. Does the employee have to comply? Is the employee entitled to additional compensation? If the employees are Hispanic and they are required to provide bilingual skills without assessment of their Spanish proficiency and without assessment of the Spanish language skills of non-Hispanics, has national origin discrimination occurred? If the bilingual Hispanics end up being assigned some of the work of non-Hispanics in addition to their own without credit or additional compensation, is that national origin discrimination? Or is an employer who requires Hispanics or any other employee to provide bilingual services merely requiring the employee to use his or her skills as necessary to meet the needs of the employer and the market?

These and many more issues will have to be resolved by employers and employees, or eventually by the courts. This is a new and developing area in "language on the job" matters. It is so new, in fact, that as of this writing (January 21, 1992), only two reported cases have gone through the trial level, several more are pending, and one appeals court decided not to reinstate a district court level case dismissed by that court. Accordingly, we are plowing new ground in this discussion. In this chapter we will consider the posture of the few cases that have been brought so far. We will then consider the broader issues with which courts and the marketplace will have to contend. Proposals for an effective resolution of these issues, as in our previous discussions, will be presented in the final chapters of this book.

Perez

On August 15, 1988 the U.S. District Court for the Western District of Texas began hearing the first-ever lawsuit involving the issue of national origin discrimination based upon forced usage of a Hispanic's bilingual abilities. Bernardo M. Perez, an FBI agent, brought the class-action suit on behalf of himself and a class of 310 persons who were or who had been special agents of the FBI. The action was brought under Title VII against the FBI and individual defendants. The trial lasted nine days. Plaintiffs in this landmark case were represented by Antonio V. Silva and Jose Angel Silva of El Paso, and by Hugo Rodriguez of Albuquerque.

In essence, after hearing the evidence, the Court concluded in the *Perez* case that Title VII had been violated by the FBI's failure to give Hispanic agents proper credit for their contributions, particularly on wire taps and undercover activities, and by their consequent exclusion from promotions and benefits. They had been selected for these assignments, the Court concluded, on the basis of language and national origin. The Court also held, however, that the business needs of the FBI had justified assignment of a disproportionate number of Hispanics to the undercover operations. In fashioning a remedy for the discrimination, the Court ordered the promotion of Perez and the convening of a three-member "special master panel" to determine the remedy of rightful place seniority for individual members of the plaintiff class. However, the Court denied the plaintiff's request to enjoin the FBI from calling upon the language skills of its agents. That, it determined, would unduly intrude upon the prerogatives of the FBI director to marshall the resources of the Bureau to perform its mission. Also, finding that Title VII remedies were only available to make plaintiffs whole and finding that Hispanic agents were not paid less than non-Hispanics, it declined to award monetary compensation for the required use of language and relied instead upon the indirect relief of the use of promotional opportunities devised by the FBI and ordered by the Court.

An examination of the factual basis underlying the Court's decision will be useful in understanding how similar cases should be treated by the courts.

At the trial of the *Perez* case, it developed that special agents enter the Bureau through one of five programs of their choice: law, language, science, accounting, or diversified. The Bureau's policy, of which candidates are informed, is that an agent's skills, ability, and expertise may be used at any and all times during an FBI career. The Court found that in practice, though, that assignments requiring language skills were particularly burdensome on Hispanic agents and significantly and negatively affected the conditions of their employment and promotional opportunities. The problem first revolved around the manner in which these language skills were identified for use by the Bureau. The Bureau, for example, indicated that special agents could not be forced to take a language exam. Under that principle, an agent who enters under the accountant or law qualification should not be required to take a language test. However, the evidence at trial led the Court to conclude that a significant number of Hispanic agents were ordered to take the language test on threat of insubordination. No persons other than Hispanics faced a similar requirement.

Another problem was the presumption by the Bureau that Hispanics would have to use their language skills even if they entered the FBI under a skill program other than language. Management of the FBI expressed its view that the FBI could not force persons who enter under an alternate qualification program to monitor Spanish-language wiretaps, but the preponderance of the evidence at trial established that Hispanic agents from all classifications had been called to monitor Spanish-language wiretaps. The Court determined that the practice of informally selecting the skills of Hispanic Spanish-speakers who entered under a program other than the language program was so widespread a practice that it became a policy of the Bureau.

Besides being required to submit to language tests even when they did not enter the Bureau under the language program, the test results themselves, the Court concluded, were highly suspect. Many of the tests were simply phone conversations lasting fifteen minutes or less. Some agents who failed a written exam were ordered on threat of insubordination to retake the exam until a passing grade was achieved. The belief was apparent that the FBI concluded that any Hispanic who did not pass the test was "faking." At the same time, Anglo counterparts were not tested for language skills. The Court determined that the FBI was not justified in presuming that too few non-Hispanic agents had a second language skill to test Anglo agents, while at the same time insisting that the vital interests of the Bureau's mission required the use of the Spanish-language skills of its Hispanic agents. This inconsistency undercut the FBI's argument that disparities in testing could be justified by reasons of business necessity. The Court also noted (in footnote twenty-five) that, "Any reason offered by the Bureau to forego testing Anglos would apply equally to Hispanics: 'There is no incentive for an agent to admit a Spanish-speaking proficiency; some will hide their ability.'"

The burden to career advancement for those agents using their Spanish-language ability became obvious at trial. Wiretaps involve long periods from eight to twelve hours during which an agent is confined or secreted in a vehicle or room listening to conversations made over a telephone. The Court determined that a wiretap is extremely difficult for the persons involved because shifts are long, the duty is not voluntary, and agents assigned to wiretaps are taken off of the active cases they have developed. Wiretap assignments also often take an agent away from his or her home for long periods. They impact negatively upon promotional opportunities because an agent whose cases are reassigned when he is forced into wiretap duty cannot "collect the ticket" when an investigation bears fruit (p. 910). Plaintiff class members testified to the existence of a widely recognized "taco circuit" or "tortilla circuit," whereby Hispanic Spanish-speaking agents were regularly chosen for thirty to ninety day assignments doing wiretap duty. Even Hispanic agents who qualified under the accountant and lawyer programs were frequently assigned to wiretaps. An agent traveling the "taco circuit" was often unavailable when special training opportunities arose and was not exposed to managers who make the subjective evaluations and determinations for career advancement. The Court found that although Title VII may not prohibit the Bureau from assigning Hispanic special agents to undercover work in disproportionate numbers, it does prohibit the Bureau from failing to credit adequately the contribution of the undercover agents to the mission of the Bureau in terms of promotions and benefits.

Buelna

On April 13, 1990 the U. S. District Court for the District of Arizona dismissed a law suit brought by Officer Arthur Buelna against the city of Chandler, Arizona. Buelna, a Hispanic police officer was assisting a police recruit who was administering a breathalyzer test to a Spanish-speaking individual. Buelna's supervisor instructed him to provide Spanish-language assistance to the recruit. Officer Buelna refused to follow the order, because he argued, he was not fluent enough to communicate meaningfully with native speakers in Spanish. He was disciplined for refusing to follow his supervisor's order. He later brought suit alleging national origin discrimination under Title VII. The defendants responded with a motion for summary judgment (a mechanism which allows a court to dismiss a case when it finds that there is no genuine issue of material fact and that the moving party should prevail as a matter of law). The district court granted the motion for summary judgment. Officer Buelna appealed.

In its decision to award summary judgment, the district court cited the *Jurado* case (see Chapter 3) for the proposition that the employer could establish a limited, reasonable, and business-related rule which requires the use of particular language by employees who could readily comply with the rule. Recall that in *Jurado*, the rule required the use of English language over the airwaves; in *Buelna*, the rule required the use of the Spanish language. *Buelna*, however, claimed that *Jurado* is distinguishable and should not apply to his case because he claimed he does not now, nor has he ever possessed the requisite Spanish-language skills needed to perform interpreting or translating functions as a police officer. He claimed that his language of preference is English, that his native language is English, that he was raised in a home in which only English was spoken. He claimed that he only possessed incipient Spanish language skills and would therefore not be fluent enough to communicate meaningfully with native speakers of Spanish. In support of his claim, Buelna underwent a language proficiency and interpretation ability evaluation on July 19, 1989. The evaluation was conducted by Roseann Duenas Gonzales. She is the director of the Federal Court Interpreter Certification Project of the graduate program in English as a Second Language at the University of Arizona. Dr. Gonzales concluded in her evaluation that because of his limited Spanish proficiency, nonexistent interpreting skills (seventh grade level), and the technical and linguistic complexity of his job as a police officer, English is the only language in which Buelna could competently perform as a police officer. Dr. Gonzales further stated that although Buelna did have occasion to use a limited amount of Spanish on the job between 1979 and 1985, he had not done so in recent years. However, the Court concluded that Buelna had a long history of providing interpretive skills and had previously received praise and commendation for providing such services. The Court concluded that Buelna did not establish a *prima facie* case of discrimination and held that his refusal of a direct order was based on his individual preference not to perform rather than on his inability to perform. The Court noted that if Buelna felt an inability, he should have nonetheless complied with the order and then followed up with an administrative grievance.

On June 18, 1991, a three judge panel of the U.S. Court of Appeals, Ninth Circuit, upheld the District Court dismissal of the case. The Ninth Circuit panel concluded that Buelna was asked to translate not because he is Hispanic but because his supervisors believed that he had demonstrated an ability to translate in the past.

In the Court's view, it made no difference whether Buelna was in fact able to translate. Buelna had offered no proof, the Court concluded, that Hispanic officers were subject to greater employment requirements in translating than non-Hispanics. Additionally, Buelna himself had conceded that he had spent many hours translating for fellow officers in the past and had received commendations for it.

This decision, however, cannot be cited as precedent under the Ninth Circuit rules for any other cases because it is listed officially as an unpublished opinion. Internally it seems to have left many issues unresolved. The factual determination as to whether Officer Buelna was able to comply with the order would appear to require a full presentation of evidence at trial rather than dismissal by summary judgment. Another issue concerns the selection of the persons required to provide interpretation. In the *Perez* case, even though the Court ultimately allowed the FBI to require Hispanic agents to use their abilities, it concluded that a "taco circuit" resulted when only Hispanic officers were required to use such skills. It also concluded that such use of skills prevented promotions and other recognition. Neither of the parties in *Buelna* disputed the fact that Chandler's duty to provide municipal services to the public requires the use of Spanish on a frequent basis. The Chandler police department determined that the way to meet that need was to require that any skills that an employee possessed be used as needed on the job, including Spanish-language skills. However, there was no evidence that Chandler had attempted to determine whether any officers other than Hispanics could provide the bilingual services. Chandler never conducted a proficiency test regarding Officer Buelna's Spanish language. Apparently because Buelna had previously tried to use his limited skills in an effort to help his employer, he would now be bound to continue to try to use those skills even if in doing so it were to the detriment of the individual for whom he was providing the service. These types of issues will ultimately need to be addressed and resolved on the appellate level in published opinions which will provide guidance to employers and employees alike.

Soriano

On January 9, 1990, the Equal Employment Opportunity Commission brought a lawsuit in U. S. District Court for the Central District of California against Contel of California, Inc. The action was brought on behalf of Paula Soriano, a Hispanic employed by Contel as a customer service representative (CSR). Ms. Soriano alleged that she was the victim of national origin discrimination because when a Spanish-speaking customer would call and receive an English-speaking CSR, the customer would be transferred to Paula Soriano or another Hispanic CSR. Ms. Soriano would be required to speak in Spanish to the customer. Yet the credit for the call would not go to the Hispanic CSR who provided the actual service, but to the CSR who first received the call. Such a system, Soriano complained, results in either lower productivity scores or extra work or both for herself and other Hispanics similarly situated. She alleged that there was no objective means of determining the identity of Spanish-speakers among Contel's CSR workers. She herself had never taken a Spanish language test, and yet Contel presumed and required her to use whatever Spanish language ability she possessed in the fashion described. Non-Hispanics were neither tested nor required to perform such translation services. She concluded that the monitoring and evaluation system was the result of either intentional disparate treatment against her and Hispanics or alternatively, was a practice that adversely impacted Hispanic employees with no supporting business justification. Moreover, she argued Contel could use alternative systems which would serve legitimate business needs of the company with lesser impact on its Hispanic employees.

When Ms. Soriano objected to the extra duties imposed in the fashion described, she was reprimanded at least three times, suspended, and escorted out of her office in a fashion she described as humiliating. She alleged that she suffered retaliation from Contel for her opposition to the system, including receiving humiliating disciplinary action and low performance ratings.

On September 26, 1990 the EEOC and Contel entered into a settlement agreement resolving many of the issues in the case.

Contel agreed to hire a Spanish-language expert qualified to devise an oral and/or written test to determine whether incumbent CSRs of Contel can perform their jobs in Spanish with the approximate equal facility that other CSRs can perform these functions in English. If a CSR is determined not to be able to perform the function in Spanish, that CSR will no longer be required to handle Spanish calls. If a CSR is determined to have adequate Spanish ability, Contel will be allowed to require the CSR to perform duties and responsibilities in the Spanish language.

Contel also agreed with the EEOC to set objective performance criteria for Spanish-speaking CSRs and non-Spanish-speaking CSRs. Contel agreed to a series of procedures for transferring customers when the customer neither speaks English nor has an interpreter. Among these procedures is the requirement that Spanish-speaking managerial or supervisory employees will be designated, and the Spanish-speaking CSR will be able to obtain assistance from that supervisor in the same manner that monolingual CSRs can obtain assistance from English-speaking supervisory employees. Both English- and Spanish-speaking customers will be contacted for quality audits; in the past, apparently only English-speaking customers were contacted by Contel. Contel also agreed that disciplinary notices and adverse references relating to performance of bilingual work will be removed from the personnel file of every CSR who has performed such work, including that of Paula Soriano. However, the agreement also provides that Contel is not required to pay a differential or any other compensation to employees for using their Spanish-speaking skills. It also explicitly recognizes that Contel may require CSRs determined to have Spanish-speaking skills to use them.

As a result of the "no compensation" provision, the Communication Workers of America did not join in the settlement. The union is now pursuing a separate action against Contel seeking compensation for Spanish-speaking CSRs.

Cota

The case of *Cota v. City of Tucson* went to trial in the U. S. District Court for the District of Arizona, in May 1991. Plaintiffs were Hispanic Spanish-speaking employees of the City of Tucson, Arizona who, by police department policy were required to use their Spanish language skills on the job. Any employee who refused to do so could receive disciplinary action, including termination. As in *Perez*, the Spanish-speaking Tucson police officers alleged they alone were given certain assignments because of their language skills, although they were not hired specifically to utilize such skills. Further, they complained that they were required to do follow-up work to incidents originally investigated by monolingual officers who were unable to complete their investigation because of language barriers. That resulted, according to the plaintiffs, in Hispanic officers receiving extra duties without compensation; meanwhile, other employees (for whom they completed investigations) did less work for the same amount of pay. As a result, they argued that providing police service to the Spanish-speaking public placed a disproportionate burden on the Hispanic officers in Tucson's police department. This fact coupled with the city's refusal to recognize and compensate the required use of Spanish language skills, they argued, is national origin discrimination contrary to Title VII. In pretrial legal proceedings, the City of Tucson had raised several defenses. One response was the argument that speaking Spanish is not a unique skill for which an officer should receive additional compensation. One of the Tucson city council members argued that if such compensation were allowed, then black officers working in predominantely black neighborhoods would have to be compensated as well. The city argued that the request of the Hispanics, if implemented, would be the equivalent of paying officers extra compensation merely because they belong to certain racial and ethnic groups.

The city council of Tucson rejected a report of the council's subcommittee on police-minority issues, which recommended that the city set up a program to compensate multilingual minority officers when they use their language skills to complete an assignment. The city maintained that testing to determine bilingual proficiency would be difficult, extra pay would give an unfair and sweeping advantage to Hispanics over all other workers (including other minority groups), and such pay for minority bilingual officers would result in excessive costs. It was also argued that if police officers were given the additional compensation, then other bilingual city employees would seek more pay for the use of their skills.

Another defense raised in the pretrial posturing was the allegation that the *Cota* plaintiffs were seeking to invoke a variation of the notion of "comparable worth." Comparable worth advocates argue that differential wage rates for predominately male and female occupations are the consequence of a subtle form of discrimination consisting of an undervaluing of traditionally female occupations. They assert that salary should be equal for jobs that are equivalent in total worth or contribution to the organization, despite possible differences between jobs and skills, effort, responsibility, or working conditions. In rejecting this type of an analysis, the Ninth Circuit opinion in the case of *AFSCME v. Washington*, 770 F.2d 1401 (9th Cir. 1985) defined comparable worth theory as postulating that sex based wage discrimination exists if employees in job classifications occupied primarily by women are paid less than employees in job classifications filled primarily by men if the jobs are of equal value to the employer, though otherwise dissimilar. (See Rossein, §7.6 for an examination of this theory.) The *Cota* plaintiffs responded by pointing out that they were not seeking to compare the worth of the jobs they perform with the worth of jobs that are not substantially equal or which are dissimilar. Instead, the *Cota* class pointed out that their claims stem from the city's refusal to compensate them for the city's own requirement that they and they alone undertake additional duties and responsibilities which others in the same job classification are not required to undertake.

On January 21, 1992, U. S. District Judge William D. Browning entered his long-awaited decision. In a forty-one page opinion, he found for the defendants. Spanish-speakers, he found, were sometimes required to use Spanish to assist people in addition to their regularly assigned work. However, he determined, such use did not detrimentally affect the Spanish speakers, nor did it result in extra work. Rather, he concluded, it resulted in different work which does not give rise to a cause of action (*Opinion and Order,* p. 12). At another point in the decision, Judge Browning determined that no member of the plaintiff class had been disciplined for refusing to speak Spanish, nor had any class member been given an involuntary assignment because of the ability of that worker to speak Spanish (p. 5). In his conclusion, the judge noted that at first blush, the conduct of which the plaintiffs complained appeared to be discriminatory. However, in this case, the evidence failed to transform the initial appearance of discrimination into a legally supportable inference of discrimination (p. 40). Plaintiffs were unable to convince this court as plaintiffs were able to do in *Perez,* that a denial of benefits of promotional opportunities was resulting from the requirement that Spanish-speaking employees use their language skills on the job.

Since any appeals from Judge Browning's ruling would lie with the U.S. Ninth Circuit, *Cota,* the *Dimaranan* and *Garcia v. Spun Steak* cases, and others (Chapter 3) could potentially allow that court to establish important guidelines in the area of language-on-the-job issues.

Questions Answered and Unanswered

As the cases described in this chapter, and others like them wind their way through the judicial system, the present state of the law seems to be that employers can require bilingual employees to use their language skills. No court has yet required that direct compensation be afforded to such employees as a result. However, if the use of the skills results in lost opportunities for promotions or positive evaluations, or if inadequate performance credit results, the employer will be found to have engaged in unlawful national origin discrimination. Assigning only Hispanics or members of other minority groups to positions requiring the use of language ability without testing nonminority workers seems to be prohibited. Similarly, a scheme that assumes–without proper testing—that all members of a minority speak the minority language or speak it sufficiently well to perform job requirements is similarly going to be treated as national origin discrimination.

However, there are many questions and issues left unresolved. For example, even though employers may require a particular bilingual employee to use his or her language skills over the employee's objection, should the employer do that? If others are available who are willing and able to perform the job function, such a requirement is only going to lead to resentment and probably lessened work performance. This may be particularly true where the employee was not informed at the time of hiring that the use of other language skills was a condition and term of the employment. In an appropriate case, such a requirement might even reach the level of breach of contract.

Another set of issues revolves around the accuracy of language testing. Without a relatively sophisticated analysis of the job requirements and an individualized attempt to determine language proficiency, it is difficult to determine how an employer could arrive at a valid conclusion as to the employee's language ability. Testing only minority group members is unlawful. In any event, even if a valid job analysis and test is created, how can it be determined whether a person "faked" the test so as to appear not to have bilingual skills? It is a waste of time and resources to thoroughly test all employees, especially when many of them legitimately and obviously have no second language skills. Would not that process ultimately also result in resentment and perhaps lower work performance?

The compensation issue is going to continue to raise many problems. Employers are going to continue to insist that they have the right to the full skills of the worker, including language abilities, without having to compensate every skill at an incremental level. For example, consider a police officer who demonstrates "superior" marksmanship skills. In the heat of a gun battle, the officer could not refuse to perform at the superior level, arguing that his coworkers were only very good marksmen. Nor is it likely he would prevail by arguing that in a gun battle he should be compensated additionally because of his superior marksmanship as opposed to only the very good marksmanship of his peers. On the other hand, greater skills are generally recognized and compensated in the work force. It is not uncommon for people with higher certifications or advanced degrees to receive compensation for these skills and abilities reflected in that additional training. Is there any reason why language should be treated any differently and go uncompensated?

Perhaps the underlying analytical problem is to determine whether language is a skill, a function of national origin, or some unique combination. If it is purely a function of national origin, then black police officers sent to a scene in a predominantely black area because their superiors conclude their presence will be more likely to calm the scene than nonblack officers should give rise to the same type of compensation and promotion arguments advanced by Hispanic police officers required to use Spanish on the job. Yet if requiring bilingual Hispanics to use Spanish without compensation is national origin discrimination, what about an Anglo-American who is bilingual—would it be national origin discrimination to require him or her to use bilingual abilities at work? If language is just a skill, do not employees have to use all skills available on the job? Or is language something different? Does it carry with it components both of a skill and also aspects of cultural identity akin to religion? Where is the boundary separating what an employee should be able to choose to sell or not sell to an employer? Is the problem really that we are trying to afford some protection to language rights under the national origin pigeonhole when it really does not analytically fit? Where does it belong? Until we amend the Equal Employment Opportunity Act and other laws, is there a way to afford protection under this pigeonhole without creating the analytical difficulties and inconsistencies facing employer, employees, and the courts? A proposed analytical (Chapter 6) and practical (Chapter 7) resolution of these issues lies ahead.

Bibliography

Books

1. Alice Kessler-Harris, *A Woman's Wage: Historical Meanings and Social Consequences* (1990).

2. Merrick T. Rossein, *Employment Discrimination Law and Litigation* (1990).

Articles

1. Tim Golden, *Tide Rises on Suits for Bilingual Work Bonuses*, N.Y. Times Law Section, May 18, 1990.

2. Ken Jennings & Robert L. Willits: *A Neglected Consideration in Sex Based Wage Discrimination Cases,* Labor Law Journal, July 1986 at 412.

3. Carlos Sanchez, *FBI Story*, Washington Post Magazine, Nov. 11, 1990.

4. Paul Weiler, *The Wages of Sex: The Uses and Limits of Comparable Worth*, 99 Harv. L. Rev. 1728 (1986).

Selected Judicial Decisions

1. *American Federation of State, County & Municipal Employees (AFSCME) v. Washington*, 770 F.2d 1401 (9th Cir. 1985).

2. *Buelna v. Chandler*, CIV 87-1499 PHX WPC (D. Ariz. 1990); 936 F. 2d 576 (9th Cir. 1991) (unpublished opinion available in Westlaw, Allfeds library).

3. *Cota v. Chandler*, CIV 85-544 TUC WDB, Opinion and Order (D. Ariz. Jan. 21, 1992).

4. *Equal Employment Opportunity Commission and Communications Workers of America v. Contel of California, Inc.*, SACV89-506–AHS (RWRX) (C.D. Cal. 1990).

5. *Perez v. FBI*, 707 F. Supp. 891 (W.D. Tex. 1988), 714 F. Supp. 1414 (W.D. Tex. 1989).

CHAPTER FIVE

UNIONIZED EMPLOYEES AND THE DUTY OF FAIR REPRESENTATION

Most of our discussion in Chapters 2–4 has concerned language issues in the context of the employer-employee relationship. No examination of language-on-the-job issues would be complete though, without considering the triangular relationships existing when non-English speaking employees are, or seek to become, members of a union. There are obvious overlaps and divergences of interests at stake among employees, unions, and employers. In this chapter we will identify those interests and examine how the courts and the National Labor Relations Board have addressed language matters. First, we will determine how non-English speaking workers have access to the initial union election. This election determines whether a particular union will be selected to act as representative for a particular group, or bargaining unit, of workers. Then, assuming a valid election has occurred and a union has been selected as representative of a bargaining unit of workers, we will consider how that union must accommodate non-English speaking workers to fulfill the duty of fair representation. In these endeavors, the reader will be referred not only to administrative and judicial decisions, but to the interpretations, analyses, and research of the foremost scholar in this field, Professor David Gregory of St. John's Law School.

Multilingual Election Materials and Union Elections

Perhaps the best way to introduce this topic is to note that a dramatic split exists between the Fifth and Seventh U.S. Circuit Courts of Appeals over the issue whether union election ballots must ever be printed in languages other than English. The U.S. Supreme Court has not addressed the issue. There is confusion in the decisions of the courts and the NLRB as to when bilingual *ballots* are required, or whether bilingual *notice* will suffice. Having noted the split in authority in this area, it is appropriate to back up and examine how the split developed.

The National Labor Relations Act (NLRA) is an extensive regulatory act that addresses labor relations in activities affecting interstate and foreign commerce. One major purpose of the Act, under Section F, is to protect interstate commerce by permitting employees to organize, bargain collectively through representatives of their own choosing, and engage in concerted activities for that and other purposes. It seeks to ensure equality of bargaining power between employers and freely chosen representatives of employees. The NLRB is given the exclusive initial power under the Act to determine whether it has jurisdiction over a particular employer in labor-related matters. It also has supervisory authority over elections to determine whether a particular labor union will be entitled to represent a group of employees. The activities of the NLRB are conducted throughout the country in various regional offices.

The NLRA does not expressly require multilingual election notices or ballots. However, as Professor Gregory notes in his 1989 *University of Cincinnati Law Review* article (cited in this chapter's bibliography), such multilingual materials may be necessary to ensure an effective and informed expression of the employees' true desires. Gregory notes that the NLRB places on the parties the burden of making a timely request for multilingual notices and ballots. In the absence of such a request, he concludes, the Board will set aside an election only if the challenging party can show the lack of bilingual materials had a markedly adverse impact on the ability of the employees to cast an informed vote. Several cases are instructive. In 1967, the NLRB set aside an election and directed a new one be held for employees of the Fibre Leather Manufacturing Corporation because fifteen to twenty of the eighty-six workers were Portuguese-speaking individuals unable to read English election notices or ballots. Bilingual observers from the NLRB were provided at the election, but they assisted only four to six Portuguese speaking employees. The Board concluded that a language handicap had adversely affected fifteen to twenty workers and that the presence of bilingual observers was not sufficient to assure the effective and informed expression by all employees of their true desire.

Later in 1967, the NLRB considered the *Trio Metal Cap Company* case. There, while the *notices* of election were printed multilingually, the *ballots* were printed only in English. The Board upheld the election. The Board announced a new position, finding that the bilingual notices assured Polish- and Spanish-speaking employees of an opportunity to make an effective and informed expression of their true desires without the need for bilingual *ballots*.

In 1969 the U. S. Fifth Circuit Court of Appeals rejected the NLRB's new position that bilingual notices alone would be sufficient. In the case of *Marriott In-Flight Services Division v. NLRB*, one-third of the employees understood only Spanish. The Board was asked to provide notices and ballots in Spanish as well as English. Election *notices* were published bilingually, but *ballots* were printed only in English. The Board held the election to be valid; the Fifth Circuit disagreed. Citing a letter written by the associate executive director of the NLRB describing Board policy, the Court noted that the letter advised that if foreign languages were used in election notices, they should also appear on the ballots. In rejecting the NLRB's argument that it had no uniform policy in this area, the Court noted that "the Board cannot, by retrospective adjudication, will away the policy that is actually being enforced by its agents and officers in day to day practice." It found that the Board's policies almost uniformly require that foreign language ballots be available when a substantial number of eligible employees do not speak English. The Fifth Circuit examined the election by applying a "minimum laboratory standard of fairness" doctrine. It found that an election necessarily falls below the minimum laboratory standards of fairness when one-third of the electorate has no access to ballots in a language it can understand. The Court stated "we can think of few things more fundamental to a democratic selection of labor representatives than the ability of the polity to cast an intelligent vote" (p. 567). It held that the party challenging the election should not have to prove actual prejudice to the outcome.

As Professor Gregory points out, the *Marriott* decision has generally not been followed by the NLRB. In 1976, the Board considered the *Norwestern Products, Inc.* case. There, the NLRB determined that, notwithstanding a severe language problem and the lack of adequate translation, a timely request for a bilingual election had not been made. The Board reaffirmed its opinion in *Marriott* (which had been rejected by the Fifth Circuit) "until such time as the Supreme Court may determine the issue." The NLRB provided in its opinion that it would "uphold stipulations by the parties as to the use of bilingual notices and ballots unless it is shown that failure to provide multilingual ballots had an adverse impact on the employees' ability to cast an informed vote." Since it found no adverse impact upon the election, it had no basis for setting aside the election. This latter statement was also a rejection of the Fifth Circuit's *Marriott* holding that the parties challenging elections should not have to prove actual prejudice. In another 1976 case, the NLRB again continued to place the burden on the challenging party. It found that a challenging party had failed to present evidence that a substantial number of Spanish surnamed employees could not read or comprehend English. Therefore, the Board concluded, the absence of bilingual ballots did not constitute sufficient grounds for setting aside the election (*Wicks Forest Industries*).

Professor Gregory cites other cases concerning multilingual election notices and ballots. In 1980, the Board set aside an election, finding that a failure to post bilingual notices as agreed constituted interference with the election (*Flo-Tronic Metal Manufacturing, Inc.*). In another case where the ballot was only in English, the election was not overturned because union members had sufficient command of the language to understand the ballot (*Long Island College Hospital v. New York State Labor Relations Board*). The Board did, however, find a ballot defective in a 1985 case. There the notices of election and instructional campaigning were considered insufficient to cure defective ballots. In that case, *Kraft Inc.*, the ballot contained four languages. Printed English and Spanish were overshadowed by hand written Vietnamese and Laotian. Moreover, the layout of the ballot made it difficult to read, even for the English reading voters. Flaws were found in the translation of the ballot's language for Vietnamese and Laotian. In 1988, however, the Board ruled that another ballot was not defective. Since only three or four voters in that case were affected by translation errors, and therefore their votes would not have changed the results of an election decided by a margin of seventy-two votes, the NLRB upheld the election in the *Bridgeport* case.

As if these decisions were not confusing enough, a split among circuits occurred with the 1990 decision of the U. S. Seventh Court of Appeals in the case of *NLRB v. Precise Castings, Inc.* In that case, a union won an election by a vote of eighteen to thirteen. There were two spoiled ballots and three challenged votes at a company where ten of the forty-one employees read and spoke only Spanish. The employer argued on behalf of the language minority employees and against the union that the ballots, which were printed only in English, prevented employees from accurately expressing their choice of bargaining representatives. Picking up on the language in *Marriott*, the company urged that only a multilingual ballot could assure the "laboratory conditions" necessary to effective choice; however, the Court disagreed. The Court first rejected the conclusion from *Marriott* that the election departed from the NLRB's policy of using bilingual ballots. It noted specifically that since *Marriott* the NLRB made it clear it had no policy requiring the use of ballots in multiple languages (citing *Norwestern Products Inc.*). The Court also determined that in any event, the laboratory conditions doctrine was based in part on a belief that labor elections should be better than political ones. It was also based on a belief that employees were easily misled and incapable of expressing their true choice except in "laboratory conditions". The Court found that since 1969 the NLRB was more likely to believe that employees could fend for themselves. The Court noted that the NLRB possesses discretion to set rules for conducting elections. Making labor elections more like political elections is among the Board's legitimate choices. The Court noted that most ballots in political elections are in English even though, as the Court conceded, the Federal Voting Rights Act requires covered jurisdictions to offer ballots in languages used by 5 percent of the populace if those groups are below the national norm in literacy. In the main, however, the Court concluded persons who do not speak English must learn from other sources how to cast an effective political vote. They must also learn, apart from the ballot, how to cast a union election vote.

Furthermore, the Court found as inapplicable the second ground of the *Marriott* decision, that elections using ballots printed in a language employees cannot understand are unfair. When the ballot appears only in English and only gives workers the options of checking a "yes" box if they favor unionization or "no" if they oppose it, the union will undoubtedly tell workers in their own tongues to check the "yes" box while the employer will instruct them to check "no". Both union and employer will use their own resources to seek to persuade in appropriate languages.

Also, the Court noted the NLRB does not leave workers to learn the pros and cons of union representation from the election campaign alone. On request of either employer or union, the NLRB will post elaborate election notices in all languages describing eligibility to vote and explaining the conduct of the election. It will also include sample ballots in the appropriate language and an explanation that the actual ballot will be printed in English. Accordingly, anyone who took the time to read the notice would be equipped to vote accurately.

The company argued that different NLRB regions currently use different procedures, which results in a lack of uniformity; however, the Seventh Circuit opinion noted that if the regions do follow different paths, then the Board would be in a better position to evaluate the results and in a better position to determine which one would be preferable. Or, it noted, the NLRB might determine that the cost and benefits of the competing options are so closely balanced that uniformity is unnecessary. Noting that the NLRB was not concerned with uniformity and that the record contained no evidence of actual confusion, the Seventh Circuit upheld the use of the English-only ballot. On April 15, 1991, the U.S. Supreme Court declined to review this case.

Despite the split between circuit courts and apparently within the NLRB regions over the use of multilingual ballots, it seems clear that if unions are to remain viable among an increasingly multilingual work force, they would want, as Professor Gregory notes, to organize all workers under the union aegis wherever possible. Political candidates of both parties have determined that appealing to voters in their native tongues is a successful strategy. It would seem only logical that union organizers would want to make the same efforts at inclusion. It is hard to see how a *Norwestern*-type agreement, whereby a union agrees that all ballots and election materials would only be printed in English, could be in the interests of a contemporary union seeking to have a majority of a heterogeneous unit vote "yes" on a union election. The only rational explanation for that type of agreement would be that the union somehow determined in advance that workers with limited English ability would vote "no" if given a fair opportunity. A conscious effort to keep those workers from voting would run afoul of even the most "hands off" approaches by the NLRB and the Seventh Circuit.

Duty of Fair Representation

Assume that a union's organizing campaign has been success-ful and a union has been selected to represent workers in a particular bargaining unit. What happens if a good many of the workers have limited English skills? What are the obligations of the union to those workers? Part of the answer lies in the judicially created Duty of Fair Representation (DFR).

In 1944 the U.S. Supreme Court announced the doctrine of DFR in the case of *Steele v. Louisville & Nashville R.R. Co.* In that case, a black locomotive fireman brought suit against his employer and the Brotherhood of Locomotive Firemen and Enginemen, which was the exclusive bargaining representative of the craft of the firemen employed by the railroad. The plaintiff brought the suit because the union, purporting to act as representative of the entire craft of firemen and without informing black firemen, sought to amend the existing collective bargaining agreement so as ultimately to exclude all black firemen from the service. On February 18, 1941 the railroads and the union entered into a new agreement which provided that not more than 50 percent of the firemen in each class of service in each seniority district of a carrier should be blacks. Further, the agreement specified that until such a percentage should be reached, all new runs and all new vacancies should be filled by white men. The agreement reserved the right of the union to negotiate for additional restrictions on the employment of black firemen. Other agreements were reached by the union that resulted in serious and adverse consequences for black firemen who were supposed to be represented by the union as their exclusive bargaining representative. The Supreme Court upheld the right of the plaintiffs to bring the action. It noted that while the majority of the craft chooses the bargaining representative, once the representative is chosen it represents the craft or class of workers and not the majority (p. 202). While the union would not have to ensure that absolutely no variations existed in the terms of contract based on differences relative to the authorized purposes, the Court specifically concluded that discrimination by the union based on race was invidious. Congress, in enacting collective bargaining legislation, did not undertake to authorize the bargaining representative to make such discrimination (p. 203). The Court stated:

> So long as a labor union assumes to act as the statutory representative of a craft, it cannot rightly refuse to perform the duty, which is inseparable from the power of representation conferred upon it, to represent the entire membership of the craft. While the statute does not deny to such a bargaining labor organization the right to deter-

mine eligibility to its membership, it does require the union, in collective bargaining and in making contracts with the carrier, to represent non-union or minority members of the craft without hostile discrimination, fairly, and impartially and in good faith. (p. 204)

In another landmark case, the U.S. Supreme Court extended the duty from the negotiation stage of collective bargaining to the administration of the negotiated agreement. In *Vaca v. Sipes* the Court determined the union breached its duty of fair representation by not taking an employee's grievance to arbitration. The Court stated:

It is now well established that as the exclusive bargaining representative of the employees . . . the union had a statutory duty fairly to
represent all of those employees, both in its collective bargaining .
. . and in its enforcement of the resulting collective bargaining
agreement . . . Under this doctrine, the exclusive agent statutory
authority to represent all members of a designated unit includes a
statutory obligation to serve the interest of all members without
hostility or discrimination toward any, to exercise its discretion with
complete good faith and honesty, and to avoid arbitrary conduct. (p.
177)

In 1983, the Court made it clear that the breach of the union's duty can create a potential for significant monetary damages. In *Bowen v. U. S. Postal Service*, the Supreme Court determined that unions would bear their portion of damages caused by failing to take a grievance to arbitration.

Beyond the judicially created duty resulting from federal labor acts, the Equal Employment Opportunity Commission has held that Title VII (see Chapter 2) creates a similar duty. The Act explicitly prohibits unlawful employment practices by labor organizations as well as employers. In a case decided in 1973, the EEOC held that the union in question had an affirmative duty to publish its collective bargaining agreement and other relevant information in both Spanish and English to meet its obligation of fair representation under Title VII. The exact parameters of the duties owed by unions under these theories, and potential incongruency in the liability, are explored in detail in two articles written and published by Professor Gregory in 1983 and 1984 (cited in the bibliography).

Returning to the language issue, a 1972 Ninth Circuit case suggests that the union's duty of fair representation includes the obligation to provide translation of the collective bargaining agreement and to furnish bilingual union representatives. Specifically, the plaintiff alleged the union breached its duty in that case by: (1) failing to provide a bilingual liaison between members of the union; (2) failing to provide a copy of the collective bargaining agreement in Spanish; (3) failing to explain to them the rights and responsibilities including the right to have the union process agreements on their behalf; and (4) failing to seek establishment of a bilingual supervisorial system that could assist union members in performance of their duties. Although the case was reversed and remanded on procedural issues, the Ninth Circuit did rule that the district court had jurisdiction to resolve the claim. The Court cited *Vaca* for the proposition that the union has a good faith duty to avoid arbitrary conduct, and also noted that this duty is a statutory duty implied by Section 9 (a) of the National Labor Relations Act as amended (29 U.S.C.A. § 1598).

In 1987, the U. S. Court of Appeals for the Ninth Circuit determined that a union was required to provide translators at monthly union meetings for Spanish-speaking members. In that case, the plaintiff belonged to Local 11 of the Hotel Employees & Restaurant Employees International Union. The plaintiff, a Mr. Zamora, did not understand English and neither did 48 percent of the 16,500 members who, like Zamora, only understood Spanish. The internal rules of the union provided for translation of collective bargaining agreements. However, at the monthly membership meetings, translation was not provided with any regularity. When translation was provided upon request, it was performed by a bilingual union officer and not an outside translator. When Zamora and others petitioned the union to provide translators at all monthly meetings, the union response was, by majority vote, to stipulate that thereafter meetings would be conducted only in English.

Zamora sued alleging a violation of Section 101 (a) (1) of the Labor Management Reporting and Disclosure Act of 1959. That provision provides:

> Every member of a labor organization shall have equal rights and privileges within such organizations . . . to attend membership meetings, and to participate in deliberations and voting upon the business of such meetings, subject to reasonable rules and regulations in such organization's constitution and bylaws.

Applying this statute, the district court ordered the union to provide a qualified translator at all monthly membership meetings to translate all debate and shop talk. The union appealed and the Ninth Circuit upheld the district court's decision. The Court determined that translation was necessary to afford equal opportunities for all union members to participate given that 48% of the union membership spoke only Spanish. While the union had insisted that the rule was mandated through democratic means (that is, a vote of the majority), the Ninth Circuit decision concluded "an undemocratic rule cannot become valid because it is adopted by democratic means" (p. 570).

Developing Sensitivity to Language Issues

Not all union-related language issues have been resolved in the courts. It may be that potential plaintiffs do not have the resources to bring challenges. Or, more likely, it may be that unions recognize that it is in their interest as well as in the interest of their members to accommodate non-English speaking workers. After all, more members means more dues and more union impact. Failure to accommodate creates the possibility of potential monetary liability imposed for breach of DFR. Additional judicial and NLRB sensitivity to the needs of persons with non-English speaking backgrounds may also be a factor. In April 1991, in the case *NLRB v. Bakers of Paris*, the U.S. Court of Appeals for the Ninth Circuit upheld an NLRB administrative law judge's decision to refuse to admit into evidence the English-language version of statements that board investigators took from non-English speaking witnesses. The employer had offered the English language statements, but the administrative law judge and the board's general counsel did not oppose the introduction of native language versions. This case is part of an emerging recognition that "English only" approaches to the conduct of union business and NLRB matters is quickly becoming a thing of the past.

In fact, Professor Gregory reports in his 1989 *University of Cincinnati Law Review* article the results of a survey of unions concerning attitudes and practices involving multilingual materials and the use of translators. Most of those unions surveyed reported that they had members of their union whose primary language is other than English or who were not fluent in English. While most had no official established policy as to how to respond to members who request the translation services, most reported that they would obtain a translator as requested. A bare majority (52 percent) of the respondents indicated that they would take unilateral steps to alleviate linguistic difficulties (pp. 168–169).

Investigations conducted by Texas Tech University law student Lawrence R. Piccagli during the 1990 fall semester also seemed to confirm a sensitivity to these issues among union officials and NLRB counsel. According to the discussions, procedural matters in over 90 percent of NLRB supervised elections held in the North Texas area have been previously agreed upon by all parties involved. Included in the agreement is whether the election will occur monolingually, bilingually, or multilingually. As a practical matter, if a union, employer, or an NLRB field worker requests a ballot in a language other than English, usually the NLRB regional director will grant the request and order the preparation and use of bilingual ballots. Even though case law seems to require that the duty is upon workers to notify the NLRB of language deficiencies, a field attorney will be sent out to inquire whether bilingual ballots and interpreters are necessary even without such requests. This is in apparent recognition of the large, and growing, Spanish speaking population in Texas. Furthermore, at the actual election all parties involved generally position multilingual observers to police the election and avoid misunderstandings. The relative sparsity of case law regarding bilingual issues, according to the NLRB attorney interviewed, is probably the result of a system that runs relatively effectively. It is routine for unions to ask for interpreters or bilingual notices, and the NLRB usually complies.

Investigation and discussion concerning the practice of unions in the Texas area similarly confirms the observation that unions are generally cooperative in accommodating multilingual workers. One union, the United Food and Commercial Workers Union, conducts meetings in both English and Spanish simultaneously, given that it has a 30 to 40 percent multilingual constituency. In another, the Operating Engineers Union Local 714 in Dallas, with approximately 15 percent Hispanic membership employs full time staff members fluent in Spanish and can also call upon their international office in Houston to send up interpreters when needed. These examples, and other union activities cited by Professor David Gregory in Chapter 1, may continue to reflect a local resolution of language issues without need to resort to the courts.

Bibliography

Articles

1. David L. Gregory, *A Call for Supreme Court Clarification of the Union Duty of Fair Representation,* 29 St. Louis U.L.J. 45 (1984).

2. David L. Gregory, *Union Leadership and Workers' Voices: Meeting the Needs of Linguistically Heterogeneous Union Members,* 58 Cinc. L. Rev. 115 (1989).

3. David L. Gregory, *Union Liability For Damages After Bowen v. Postal Service: The Incongruity Between Labor Law and Title VII Jurisprudence,* 35 Baylor L. Rev. 237 (1983).

4. Michael C. Harper and Ira C. Lupu, *Fair Representation As Equal Protection,* 98 Harv. L. Rev. 1211 (1985).

5. Lawrence Piccagli, *Union Representation of the Non-English-Speaking Worker,* (Nov. 1990), unpublished student paper, Tex. Tech Univ. Law School, (on file with this author).

Selected Judicial and Administrative Decisions

1. *Bowen v. U. S. Postal Serv.*, 459 U.S. 212 (1983).

2. *Bridgeport Fittings*, 288 NLRB 124, 127 LRRM (BNA) 1289 (1988).

3. *Fibre Leather Mfg. Corp.* 167 NLRB 393, 66 LRRM (BNA) 1056 (1967).

4. *Flo-Tronic Metal Manufacturing, Inc.*, 251 NLRB 1546, 105 LRRM (BNA) 1144 (1980).

5. *Kraft, Inc.*, 273 NLRB 1484, 118 LRRM (BNA) 1242 (1985)

6. *Marriott In-Flight Servs. Div. v. NLRB,* 417 F.2d 563 (5th Cir. 1969), *cert. denied* 397 U.S. 920 (1970).

7. *NLRB v. Bakers of Paris,* 137 LRRM 2007, CA 9, No. 89-70050, April 8, 1991, cited in 13 LRR 6 (May 6, 1991).

8. *NLRB v. Precise Castings, Inc.,* 915 F.2d 1160 (1990), *cert. denied* 111 S.Ct. 1581 (1991).

9. *Norwestern Products, Inc.*, 226 NLRB 653, 93 LRRM (BNA) 1322 (1976).

10. *Retana v. Apartment Operators Local 14,* 453 F.2d 1018 (9th Cir. 1972).

11. *Steele v. Louisville & Nashville R.R. Co.,* 323 U.S. 192 (1944).

12. *Trio Metal Cap Co.,* 168 NLRB 802, 66 LRRM (BNA) 1382 (1967).

13. *Unibilt Industries, Inc.,* 278 NLRB 825, 121 LRRM (BNA) 1240 (1986).

14. *Vaca v. Sipes,* 386 U.S. 171 (1967).

15. *Zamora v. Local 11, Hotel Employees & Restaurant Employees Int'l Union,* 817 F.2d 566 (9th Cir. 1987).

16. Commission Decision No. 73–0377, 19 Fair Empl. Prac. Cas. (BNA) 1776 (EEOC 1972).

Labor Statutes

1. National Labor Relations Act of 1935, ch. 372, 49 Stat. 449 (current version at 29 U.S.C. section 151 (1988)) (also known as the Wagner Act).

2. Labor-Management Relations Act of 1947, ch. 120, 61 Stat. 136 (current version at 29 U.S.C. section 141 (1988)) (also known as the Taft-Hartley Act).

3. Labor-Management Reporting and Disclosure Act of 1959, Pub. L. No. 86–257, section 2, 73 Stat. 519 (current version at 29 U.S.C. section 401 (1988)) (also known as the Landrum-Griffin Act).

Part Three

STRIKING THE
BALANCE

CHAPTER SIX

Reexamining the Approach of the Legal System

Part One of this book considered language-on-the-job issues from the perspective of historical issues and contemporary approaches tied to demands of the marketplace. In Part Two we examined legal remedies in rulings on these matters by courts and administrative bodies. In this Part, having now considered the issues and remaining unresolved problems, we propose how the legal system (Chapter 6) and the marketplace (Chapter 7) might better respond to language issues.

The first step must be to reexamine existing legal approaches to make sure they fairly take into account the legitimate interests at stake. The rulings must be able to provide all parties with predictability. Otherwise, ad hoc, inconsistent decisions will only lead to more litigation. The legal system must be able to give the marketplace sufficient guidance as to parameters so that resort to the state through its courts becomes a rare occurrence. After all, the interests of employer, employee, and union should have at least the common goal of attracting and retaining competent employees who are compensated at a fair rate. Resources diverted from this common goal into litigation can only reduce the resources ultimately available to individual workers, management, owners, and unions. This is not to say that the adversary process should never be invoked; indeed, the availability of this not-so-civilized form of combat makes alternatives attractive. In this chapter we will focus on identifying how courts and legislatures should begin to approach language-on-the-job issues. These approaches, this author suggests, would provide a model for equitably resolving the legal disputes, which will inevitably continue to arise.

How Should the Legal System View Language?

At least part of the uncertainties in attempting to formulate predictable legal guidelines for language-on-the-job issues has to do with the unresolved legal status of language itself. Language is obviously a skill, but it is something more than that. From a sociological-linguistic point of view, it is more than a neutral tool for communication of ideas. It is, instead, at least according to some, a perspective or a world view. It shapes the thoughts of its users and, in a manner similar to religion, affects people's perceptions of events and their meanings. It is an inseparable aspect of culture. Language choice and the enforcement of that choice represent attempts to subordinate one culture to another.

Yet, despite this complex function of language, when it becomes a factor in judicial or legislative determinations, it appears under the categories of race or national origin. In the past, this author has demonstrated the inconsistencies flowing from the efforts of courts and legislatures when language operates as a barrier to access to legal rights, such as the right to defend oneself in a criminal prosecution. Similarly, cases involving access to basic human needs, such as education and public assistance programs, founder when language issues are raised. Until the advent of a more comprehensive jurisprudence, based upon an analysis of the underlying interests at stake, courts, legislatures, and parties and their attorneys will be required to follow the traditional approach of examining the cases and applicable laws, applying those that are useful and attempting to distinguish those that are not. The most recent pronouncement by the U.S. Supreme Court on language issues highlights the uncertainties that will inevitably flow from forcing language rights into a narrow pigeon-hole rather than focusing on the impact on underlying interests.

On May 28, 1991 the U.S. Supreme Court announced its opinion in the case of *Hernandez v. New York,* in which the prosecutor in a New York criminal trial had used peremptory challenges to exclude two potential Latino jurors who were bilingual. They were stricken, according to the prosecutor, because they had looked away from him and hesitated before responding affirmatively to the prosecutor's inquiry whether they would accept a translator as the final arbiter of some witness's responses which were going to occur in Spanish and be translated into English. Previous Supreme Court decisions and a federal statute (Civil Rights Act of 1875, now 18 U.S.C. §243) make it unlawful to remove jurors from a criminal prosecution on the basis of race. In fact, in an opinion handed down less than two months prior to its *Hernandez* decision, the Court found that a white defendant was denied equal protection when African-Americans were excluded from the jury. In that case, *Powers v. Ohio*, Justice Kennedy wrote as part of the majority opinion that "racial discrimination in the qualification or selection of jurors offends the dignity of persons and the integrity of the courts (59 U.S.L.W. 4268 at 4269, 4/2/91). With the exception of voting, he concluded, "for most citizens the honor and privilege of jury duty is their most significant opportunity to participate in the democratic process" (59 U.S.L.W. at 4270, 4/2/91).

Justice Kennedy also wrote the majority opinion in *Hernandez*. He noted, with apparent approval and citing noted sociological and linguistic experts, the complex function of language:

> Language permits an individual to express both a personal identity and membership in a community, and those who share a common language may interact in ways more intimate than those without this bond. Bilinguals, in a sense, inhabit two communities, and serve to bring them closer. Indeed, some scholarly comment suggests that people proficient in two languages may not at times think in one language to the exclusion of the other. The analogy is that of a high-hurdler, who combines the ability to spring and to jump to accomplish a third feat with characteristics of its own, rather than two separate functions. Grosjean, The Bilingual as a Competent but Specific Speaker-Hearer, 6 J. Multilingual & Multicultural Development 467 (1985). This is not to say that the cognitive processes and reactions of those who speak two languages are susceptible of easy generalization, for even the term "bilingual" does not describe a uniform category. It is a simple word for a more complex phenomenon with many distinct categories and subdivisions. Sanchez, Our Linguistic and Social Context, in Spanish in the United States 9, 12 (J. Amastae & Elias-Olivares 1982); Dodson, Second Language Acquisition and Bilingual Development: A Theoretical Framework, 6 J. Multilingual

& Multicultural Development 325, 326-327 (1983). (59 U.S.L.W. at 4506)

Then, however, in this author's opinion, the Supreme Court halted what appeared to be the first steps toward identifying the real issues. It did not consider the extraordinary thing being asked of bilingual jurors: that if they hear words in Spanish, which bring some images to mind, they must somehow forget those images and thoughts and accept only the images and thoughts raised by the English language version offered by the interpreter. Because the Court did not consider what an extraordinary request was being made, it jumped to the conclusion that the hesitance justified their removal. If the Court *had* understood the nature of the request, it might have concluded that hesitancy is the only honest reaction from a layperson who is asked to put aside the first images and version of reality in absolute favor of a second, potentially inaccurate rendition. The Court also might have focused on the importance of the honor and privilege of jury duty for bilingual citizens, and of the integrity of the courts, in accordance with its *Powers* decision. It might have considered the fact that if all attorneys, witnesses, and other jurors are monolingual, the only person in the courtroom who would know if a translation error had occurred would be a bilingual juror. Yet, that juror is sworn to apparently ignore the error. He or she would never have the chance to serve as a juror unless he or she unhesitatingly promises not to reveal any translation errors to the court. Instead of focusing on the real interests of guaranteeing that the truth prevails in trials and that bilingual citizens can participate in our democracy as jurors, the Court upheld the conviction and the decision in *Hernandez* to exclude the bilingual jurors. It concluded it need not address Hernandez's argument that Spanish-speaking ability bears such a close relation to ethnicity that exercising a peremptory challenge on the basis of language violated the equal protection clause, because the prosecutor had explained that the jurors' specific responses and their demeanor, and not their language proficiency alone caused him to doubt their ability to defer to the official translation. The Court noted that the lower court could have relied on the fact that the prosecutor defended his use of peremptory challenges without being asked to do so by the judge, that he did not know which jurors were Latinos, and that the ethnicity of the victims and the prosecution witnesses (Latinos) tended to undercut any motive to exclude Latinos from the jury. However, the Court noted that it might be, for certain ethnic groups in some communities, that proficiency in a particular language is akin to skin color in its consequences and therefore should be treated as a surrogate for race under equal protection analysis. Is discrimination on the basis of language an instance of national origin or racial discrimination? The Supreme Court's answer is that maybe it can be, depending upon the circumstances. But the better inquiry would have been to determine the effect on the dignity of witnesses and jurors and the consequences for the integrity of the courts. The virtual automatic exclusion of bilingual jurors in this case is an effect that must be addressed regardless of the ethnicity of victims and witnesses and regardless of whether there could be a showing of intentional racial discrimination on the part of the prosecutor.

The same type of deficiency occurs in the employment context where courts generally fail to consider that everyone has an accent and uses language at a different level of skill and sophistication. Instead, the inquiry becomes whether the employer is trying to impose burdens on national origin groups. This analysis becomes even more confounding to an observer who notes that many of the members of the differing national origin groups involved in the discussions were born in this country as were their recent ancestors.

Until legislatures, regulatory agencies, and the courts change the focus, the task facing those interested in the resolution of language issues will be to take the cases and the analysis (presented in Chapters 2 through 5) and apply them where possible, and distinguish them where necessary. The linkage between language and race or national origin has acquired so much inertia in so many areas of the law that immediate change is unlikely. Further, until the change occurs, this author would not recommend removing the limited, if analytically unsound, protection that these statutes and decisions afford. However, legislatures and courts should begin rethinking these issues and trying to identify the real issues at stake. In general, and as a beginning, they might consider the following approach, which incorporates current analysis and a discussion of the impact of impermissible preferences upon a free market economy.

What is essentially at issue in the hiring or promotion cases (Chapter 2) is the right of an employee from a multicultural background to enter into an employment contract for a position for which he or she is otherwise qualified, free of the limitation that the ability of that worker to communicate in more than one language could be a legally sufficient reason to disqualify employment or deny promotion. In the communication among employee cases (Chapter 3), the issue should be seen as whether such an employee can be required to waive the right to communicate in a manner which has been acquired through the individual's cultural upbringing. If the business needs of the employer require multilingual skills (Chapter 4), the concern should be whether the agreement between employer and employee includes the understanding that such is a term of the agreement and that such a provision, express or implied, is supported by consideration as would be sufficient to uphold any other contract. The union election and representation cases (Chapter 5) should turn upon deciding whether workers are being denied the exercise of their right to organize and bargain collectively and be represented because the union chooses to conduct business in a language that effectively prevents the participation of workers who have not yet acquired skills in that tongue.

With this as an overview, we turn to a reexamination of the approaches to the legal issues raised by preceding chapters.

Reexamining Hiring and Promotion Cases (Chapter 2)

This author suggests that courts reexamine how language is acquired, its relation to cultural identity, and conduct a critical examination of impermissible bias masking as a claim of unintelligibility.

For most people, language is a reflection of cultural contacts and upbringing acquired from a very early age. The exception would be language skills acquired later in life and used only as "second language" skills. As a result, for those who acquire a language at an early age, it forms an immutable perspective and understanding. It does not appear that human beings can consciously purge themselves of this perspective. For courts to suggest otherwise is absurd. For example, consider an individual who has learned from infancy that the word *madre* represents the female adult who gave him or her birth. If that person is called to court as a juror and told by an incompetent translator that *madre* means *cloud* or some other word, the juror will not be able to stop the neurological processes that bring the image of mother to mind. Similarly, when the same individual presents himself or herself for employment, that worker would not be able to purge himself or herself of native language abilities even if he or she wanted to. The worker could not change the neurological processes that had been set in place from a very early age. Many cultural and linguistic manifestations share identifiable national origins. However, in many instances culture and language are fluid, vibrant matters. The recent communication explosion, coupled with political and economic events, means that language usage, particularly Spanish, has spilled across national borders. Thus no absolute correlation exists between language ability and the national origin of an individual or the individual's ancestors. But to those who have acquired language skills at an early age from other members of an identifiable culture, while the language skills may wither to some extent if not practiced, they are not consciously "mutable" in the same way that a person could willfully change hairstyles.

As a corollary to the notion that culturally acquired language skills may be immutable is the phenomenon of accent. Human beings have an obvious ability to learn more than one language. When they learn a second one, they apparently carry over some of the pronunciation patterns to the second. Particularly among older persons, the accent may be practically immutable. The accent is a signal to the listener that the speaker has multilingual abilities. To some, that signal is a positive one. This author was taught in New

Mexico at an early age that if someone speaks with a foreign accent, respect should be shown because the person is intelligent and educated enough to know more than one language. Others, however, may view the accent negatively depending on its nature. European language accents may be looked upon as a mark of intelligence and distinction, while others may constitute a mark of inferiority. An authority on Native-American law in New Mexico, Carey N. Vicenti, cautions fellow attorneys to expect and accept accents in tribal courts:

> An American in a French court would have as many difficulties as if he or she were in an Indian Court, but we tend to forgive the French because we know of their history and we give them credit that they have accomplished the merit badge of high culture. Yet, the French will not struggle to conduct their court in English, although Indian courts will. And when we hear the broken English and the accent of an Indian Judge or advocate, we assume that he or she is unintelligent, although we would never do that to Henry Kissinger. (Prologue, N.M. Indian Tribal Court Handbook)

The *Giles* article cited in the bibliography contains a detailed study of ethnocentrism and the evaluation of accented speech. As Matsuda notes, citing Eisenstein, this attitude toward particular accent affects the listener's perception of the speaker's intelligibility. She notes that the unintelligibility claim in effect masks a preference claim which translates "I cannot tolerate differences" (p. 1379). This preference may also mask notions of racial and cultural dominance.

Courts should be sensitive to the possibility that this hidden preference is being used to prevent an otherwise qualified worker from entering into an employment contract or serving as the basis for denial of a promotion. They should examine their own attitudes when the worker presents himself or herself, accent and all, in court. Instead of hearing the accent and concluding that the accent confirms that the employer was truthful and the worker unqualified, courts should go farther. They should require an inquiry into the possibility that the employer is seeking to impose an impermissible preference. They should consider that, in effect, the worker is being denied the opportunity to enter into a contract because of multiple language abilities. They should scrutinize claims of unintelligibility or claims that a particular job requires an artificially inflated level of English-language skills. Courts should even consider and recognize, as in the *Gutierrez* case (Chapter 3) that multiculturalism is one of this country's greatest strengths. So, too, is a free market economy where workers are allowed to contract in their interest to provide the labor necessary for the functioning of the economy. An employer who seeks to subvert these strengths by denying a multicultural worker the right to contract for his or her labor damages not only the individual worker but potentially the entire economic system. Workers, such as *Fragante,* lose the opportunity to contract not because of a lack of objective qualifications, but because of the subjective monocultural preference of a potential employer. Upholding that preference means that the highest scoring applicant is unavailable to furnish his skills to the society which otherwise would benefit from them. No inquiry was made in the *Fragante* case of potentially available means to overcome any perceived oral deficiencies. Neither was consideration given to the fact that up until now, customer preference based on otherwise impermissible bases has not been considered a legally sufficient justification to interfere with the right of an employee to contract for his or her labor. For example, a customer preference for female flight attendants was held insufficient justification for refusal by an airline to hire men for the same jobs (*Diaz v. Pan Am Airways*). Catering to prejudice, it has been observed, out of fear of provoking greater prejudice only perpetuates racism (*Hernandez v. Erlenbusch*).

Courts should probe closely under existing statutes to determine whether claims of unintelligibility or that a job requires a high level of English-language skill mask national origin or race discrimination. Eventually courts and legislatures should consider the historical reality, as set forth in Chapter 1, that accommodating workers from different linguistic and cultural backgrounds has been a strength of our economic system. Failure to accommodate will weaken it. The IRCA sanctions should be repealed because they add to discrimination, interfere with contractual rights of workers, and ultimately will strip from our economy foreign looking and sounding workers together with their vitality and skills.

Reexamining Communication Among Employee Cases (Chapter 3)

It is difficult to add to the enlightened view in the *Gutierrez* decision of the cultural rights of workers. If anything can be added to the analysis, it would be. In the hiring and promotion cases, cultural and racial bias mask as a claim of job incompetence. The multilingual worker, it is alleged, is unable to perform the job to the employer's standards because of language deficiencies. The cases involving communication among workers afford even less pretextual defense to the employer seeking to impose monoculturalism. After all, no claim is made that the use of another language precludes job competence. Rather, the issue is almost exclusively one of cultural preference. The real preference is that of the employer, but it masks as the preference of co-workers (*Gutierrez*) or customers (*Garcia*).

Courts should be more willing to look behind the masks. Obviously a private business seeks to make a profit. It does so, in part, by satisfying the consumer needs of its customers. Employers must be free to determine how best to satisfy the consumer needs, including the need of the purchaser to obtain information from the agents or employees of the employer. However, while some concerns of the customer legitimately relate to the quality of the product or service, traditionally we have recognized societal limits on the claims of legitimacy. We do not believe it is a valid consumer need to have women rather than men serve as airline attendants (*Diaz*). Similarly, we do not believe it is legitimate for a consumer to limit the employer's agent because of preferences based on race, national origin, or religious background. In effect, as a matter of national policy, we have determined that business does not have a right to make a profit at the expense of violations of workers' rights to be free from impermissible discrimination.

The preference of workers for monocultural coworkers runs afoul of the same concerns. Additionally, it may be a cynically provoked attempt to pit workers of minority backgrounds against one another in an attempt to create the very divisiveness that might then be invoked as a justification for the imposition of monocultural language rules. The preference stems from a fear of the unknown–the persistent fear of some monolinguals that speakers of other languages are talking about them. Courts should unmask this type of justification by inquiring how it is that the monolingual concludes the topic concerns him or her. Also, courts should examine what rules, if any, exist to prevent coworkers from talking about each other in English and how such rules could ever be enforced.

Mutability again raises its head in this discussion. The *Garcia* approach would uphold restrictive speak-only-English rules on the theory that language is mutable, and because therefore the bilingual employee can choose to speak the language which the employer prefers. In this context, language *is* generally mutable. Bilingual employees probably can consciously choose to use one language instead of another. (I say "probably" because it is this bilingual author's experience that in some circumstances the first words that come to mind are occasionally Spanish ones. This subjective observation is confirmed in the scholarly works cited by Justice Kennedy in the *Hernandez* case.)

But that analysis begs the question as to why the employer's monocultural preference should legally prevail over the multilingual employee's language choice. What is it that the employee has sold to the employer? After all, religion is mutable yet we would not hesitate to conclude the employer should not be allowed to force an employee to change his or her world view as molded by religion. Why should an employee be forced to surrender his or her right to communicate with coworkers who share a similar cultural world view in the language of that culture, at least where no immediate danger to person or property is at stake? Even where safety concerns are raised, courts should consider whether those concerns are legitimate or instead are pretexts that mask cultural oppression.

Reexamining Cases Involving Required Multilingual Communication with Customers (Chapter 4)

The traditional contracts approach requires, in general, that for a purported agreement to be enforceable there must be mutual assent (express or implied) and it must be supported by consideration.

In the language cases that have arisen so far, it is assumed that the employer has the right to the use of a bilingual employee's language abilities, even in the absence of any evidence that the employee in any manner assented to sell that skill to the employer. Given the unique status of language as both a skill and a function of culture and national origin, courts should require proof that the employee has agreed to sell linguistic/cultural skills to the employer before requiring employee performance. Not all multilingual employees want to sell those skills. Some of them, out of concern over their own skill level, find such a requirement of use of bilingual skills to be too burdensome. Others, the victims of discrimination, may choose not to publicly identify with the culture that is still the target of oppression. However distasteful to some this conscious decision not to identify with a minority culture might be, the employee's choice should be respected.

Of course, this is not to say that employers could not, in advance, make the use of such abilities a specific term of an employment contract. Indeed, to accommodate market concerns the employer may have to furnish information regarding products in a language the customer understands. Use of consenting multilingual employees may be the only practical way to meet this need.

A diversion is important here. We have already concluded that customer preference based upon illegitimate concerns including race and national origin, should not justify language restriction. Bilingual employees, we discussed, should not have to avoid communicating in a foreign language among themselves because a monolingual customer objects. Under the traditional view, customers cannot insist on being attended to only by representatives selected on the basis of gender, race, or national origin. Should a customer's preference to be waited on in a foreign language be considered, in effect, impermissible national origin discrimination? If language always equals national origin, the answer would have to be "yes". Such would be impermissible national origin discrimination. But as noted, and as is illustrated in this hypothetical example, language and national origin are not exactly the same concept. Non-Hispanics, for example, can learn to speak Spanish and fulfill Spanish-speaking customers' preferences and needs. While a customer's preference for communication with an employee in a particular language is legitimate, the customer's preference to be attended by an employee based solely on the national origin of that employee is not. Therefore, courts should rule as impermissible an employer's refusal, for example, to hire a non-Hispanic based upon a customer's preference for Hispanics. But, courts should uphold an employer's hiring of a person selected because of foreign language ability to satisfy a customer preference to be waited on in that language, just as they should uphold an employer's requirement that employees speak English at a legitimate and appropriate skill level in order to attend to monolingual English-speaking customers. If a customer wishes to discuss the goods and services in Spanish, employers should be free to refer a bilingual worker who has agreed to furnish those skills. Such an arrangement addresses the consumer's concerns and protects the economic interests of the employer and his or her business and profits.

Assuming that the employer needs the skills of bilingual employees and those employees have assented, the inquiry should not end there. Courts should reexamine the compensation issues as well. That is, they should explore whether some benefit has been conferred upon the bilingual speaker by the employer in return for the furnishing of language skills. Courts generally will not look to the adequacy of the consideration, but they will find contracts unconscionable where there is no value at all given in return for the promise. In the language context, employers might argue that the consideration is the salary paid for performance of the job. But if the bilingual worker has to provide all of the work skills and satisfy all of the job requirements of monolinguals in the same category, and beyond that, furnish language skills, courts should conclude that no consideration exists for the use of the language skill and therefore no obligation exists to provide it. Or, where the employee willingly provides the skill, courts should require payment of its fair value depending upon the nature and frequency of use. Lost opportunities for promotion and profit should also be compensated (*Perez*). Fair testing and evaluation of all employees who choose to participate in language skills positions should be made available. The burdens and benefits should not fall only on one national origin group to the exclusion of others.

Reexamination of Union Election and Representation Cases (Chapter 5)

The workers who are the subjects of this discussion are clearly competent, as determined by employers, to perform their jobs notwithstanding potential language difficulties. Resolution of these cases should turn upon a court determining whether workers are being denied the federally guaranteed right to organize and bargain collectively and be represented because the union in question chooses to conduct business in a language that effectively prevents the participation of workers who have not yet acquired skills in that tongue. In approaching these cases and determining what level of communication of materials or ballots is necessary, courts should not ignore the reality that Hispanics, and particularly Mexican-Americans, have long been the victims of educational discrimination. Unlike other immigrant groups, Hispanics, particularly those in agricultural work, have long been excluded from language, literacy, and training programs. A U.S. Census Bureau report, cited in the April 11, 1991 edition of the *Dallas Morning News* notes that Hispanic workers tend to be concentrated in low wage service jobs or as laborers. Their earnings trail non-Hispanic incomes. Twenty-one percent of Hispanic children are poor, compared with 11 percent of all U.S. children. A March 1989 publication of the U.S. Bureau of the Census "The Hispanic Population of the United States" (p.20 No. 444, 1989) notes that among non-Hispanics in the United States, 78.8 percent of persons twenty-five years or older had attended four years of high school while only 50.9 percent of Hispanics noted the same accomplishment. In considering poverty rates, 9.4 percent of non-Hispanic families fell below the poverty level while 23.7 percent of Hispanics were in this category. Another study by the National Council of La Raza, entitled *The Education of Hispanics: Status and Implications*, cited in *Valencia*, notes that Hispanic adults typically have higher functional illiteracy rates, in some cases up to 56 percent, compared to African-Americans (44 percent) and Anglos (16 percent). Accordingly, a mere literal translation of election materials and ballots may keep the Hispanic worker with a language barrier from effective participation in union matters. Courts should not permit the existence of the unfortunate situation where a worker overcomes hurdles and convinces the employer of work competence only to surrender the right to effective representation at the hands of a union's cultural preference policy.

Concluding Observations on the Use of the Adversary System

The unsettled nature of the law and changing demographics suggest that language-on-the-job issues will continue to surface. The limitation inherent in approaching these matters only from a legal perspective is that the focus will be on attempting to predict how courts will rule on prospective cases based upon past ones. This approach to resolution of language-on-the-job issues is inherently slow and expensive. It relies upon the willingness and ability of litigants to bring these issues into an adversary clash. Money and time needed for court challenges are two obvious limitations to this method of resolution. What may not be as obvious, but is nonetheless critical, is the ill will generated in the process. No defendant involved in a case brought by this author has ever thanked him for bringing the lawsuit. Plaintiffs, even victorious ones, are never really made whole for the tremendous financial and emotional burdens of litigation.

There will be occasions when resorting to litigation becomes a necessity. Among the advantages afforded by the adversary system is that precedent can be set and applied. The dispute is resolved in public. The process does not rely on the voluntary participation of those satisfied with the status quo: the unempowered can force the powerful to explain and justify their actions. (Each of these "pluses" can also be a negative, of course, depending upon the perspective and circumstances of the parties.)

In most situations, however, the costs associated with litigation make it too inefficient, too ineffective, and too damaging to long-term relationships. This should hold particularly true in the employment area where the ongoing interests of employer, employee, and union need to have at least some common ground.

If these language issues are going to continue to surface, and if litigation is generally going to be too costly in terms not only of economics but also in terms of human relations, effective resolution of differences must come by exploring and developing alternative recourses. That will be our next, and last, discussion.

Bibliography

Articles

1. C. J. Dodson, *Second Language Acquisition and Bilingual Development: A Theoretical Framework*, 6 J. Multilingual & Multicultural Development 325 (1985).

2. Miriam Eisenstein, *Native Reactions to Non-native Speech: A Review of Empirical Research*, 5 Studies in Second Language Acquisition 160 (1983).

3. Howard Giles, *Ethnocentrism and the Evaluation of Accented Speech*, 10 Brit. J. Soc. & Clinical Psychology 187 (1971).

4. Francois Grosjean, *The Bilingual as a Competent but Specific Speaker-Hearer*, 6 J. Multilingual & Multicultural Development 467 (1985).

5. Bill Piatt, *Attorney as Interpreter: A Return to Babble*, 20 N.M.L. Rev. 1 (1990)..

6. *Report Cites Hispanic Woes*, The Dallas Morning News, April 11, 1991, at 10A.

7. Rosaura Sanchez, *Our Linguistic and Social Context*, in Spanish in the United States 9, 12 (Jon Amastae & Lucia Elias-Olivarez 1982).

8. Reynaldo Anaya Valencia & Rodolfo Rodriguez, Jr., *Political Empowerment Under Section 2 of the Voting Rights Act of 1965 as a Route to Higher Educational Achievement: The Unrealized Dream for Texas Hispanics* (May 3, 1990) (unpublished manuscript available on file with the author).

Selected Judicial Decisions

1. *Hernandez v. New York,* 111 S. Ct. 1859 (1991).

2. *Powers v. Ohio,* 111 S. Ct. 1364 (1991).

Other Authorities

1. National Council of La Raza, *The Education of Hispanics: Status and Implications*, cited by Valencia at 9.

2. *New Mexico Indian Tribal Court Handbook,* Continuing Legal Education and the Indian Law Section of the State Bar of New Mexico (1991).

3. U.S. Bureau of the Census, "The Hispanic Population in the United States: March 1989," *Current Population Reports*, P–20, No. 444.

CHAPTER 7

Models for Accommodation

Perhaps even more important than courts and legislatures should be the marketplace itself in resolving language-on-the-job issues. Participants should be able to identify when overly restrictive language policies hinder earning profits or providing services, and in such situations they can make quicker corrections than can courts.

The efficiency of the marketplace in language rights issues has been most effectively demonstrated to this author in the realm of broadcasting. In that area, the Federal Communication Commission has never required broadcasters to provide foreign language broadcasting. However, it has required that broadcasting be made in the public interest. The U.S. Supreme Court has upheld the FCC's decision to give preference to minority ownership to increase diversity in broadcasting. However, courts and the FCC have been ambivalent in deciding whether foreign language broadcasting was necessary or even desirable. This author has urged, so far unsuccessfully, that Congress, the FCC, and the courts explicitly recognize a right in the broadcast audience to foreign language programming under certain circumstances, and a concomitant obligation of broadcasters to provide it. In the meantime, the market has acted. There is an obvious profit to be made by appealing to a mushrooming Spanish-language audience in their tongue. The legal system may eventually get around to recognizing what the market already understands: a growing segment of this country's population wants Spanish-language broadcasting. Broadcasting is entertainment, but it is much more than that. It provides positive self-images for Hispanics who now see themselves in the same sitcoms, soaps, and news broadcasts as the majority audience. It gives them the understanding of issues critical to their participation in this democracy, including the ability to cast a more informed vote and to more effectively exercise other rights. The market has acted.

The examples cited in the last section of Chapter 1 suggest that in many instances the market has also jumped ahead of the legal system in identifying and resolving language rights issues on the job. Enlightened managers, unions, and employees should, in fact, in this free market economy be the primary decision makers in these matters. This chapter provides some initial suggestions for accommodating the competing and concurrent interests identified throughout this book. It is only a starting point; employees and managers with much more experience than this author in resolving language-on-the-job issues will undoubtedly be able to identify many more models for accommodation in their particular circumstances.

Creating Models

It is always easier to plan for and prevent problems from developing than to try to resolve conflict after it has arisen. The logical first step would be to develop a method to anticipate potential language problems and resolve them prospectively. In the area of hiring and promotion, an objective audit of the level of language skills actually needed to perform job requirements could be conducted. The evaluation would be sensitive to the conscious or subconscious culture bias that could tend to produce an artificially high level of English proficiency in a job description.

For those positions where English usage is one of only many skills needed, employers should establish programs that afford employees an opportunity to apply all remaining skills to the mutual use of the firm while the English language skills of the employee are developed. The wheel does not have to be reinvented in this regard. Large firms could follow the historical and contemporary approach of providing on-site language training.

Smaller firms can take advantage of community language education programs. Professor Gregory notes (p. 127) that South East Community College in Lincoln, Nebraska offers many fundamental literacy programs for local employers' workers, with financing of instructors and materials provided by the U. S. government's Adult Basic Education Program. Many Hispanic leaders have long urged that the Federal Job Training Partnership Act include language training as part of its attempt to produce skilled workers. Dr. W. Ann Reynolds, Chancellor of the City University of New York, is seeking to implement a College Preparatory Initiative, with support from the private sector. She feels the private sector would be one of the prime beneficiaries of a program that would supplement English-language proficiency educational programs in the New York high schools. Many social service and volunteer agencies, to assist immigrants in fulfilling their English-language requirements necessary to obtain citizenship in the United States have initiated English language programs. So far, organizations like U.S. English and English First have devoted time and resources to counterproductive attempts to create and impose official English laws. If they ever seriously decided to promote the use of the English language, they would realize that they could convert their hitherto counterproductive scare campaigns into a positive effort by establishing English-language training programs for the workers whose foreign tongues they fear so much.

Successful completion of English-language training programs could, if explicitly agreed to up-front by employer and employee and if required for actual job performance, become one of the requirements for an employee's retention and promotion.

Individual job needs vary. Accordingly, it would be impossible to create a blanket accommodation scheme that would fairly take into account every job or employment position. But management, with the help of experienced consultants, could come up with creative methods of accommodation in conjunction with the English-language training programs.

Take, for example, the occupation of cab driver. Market conditions seem to permit people with limited English-speaking abilities to become cab drivers, particularly in metropolitan areas. This phenomenon was noted humorously by Mark Russell in a PBS presentation in April 1991. He observed that only in America can a person arrive here speaking no English and the next day become a cab driver. The non–English-speaking cab driver also became the focus of humor and a mix-up in Bill Murray's 1989 movie "Quick Change". If the market is producing cab drivers with limited English skills, and if there is a need to address these issues, one accommodation scheme would be as follows. Suppose that a cab driver is being hired, and that the applicant possesses to a very satisfactory degree the skills of driving ability, honesty, physical stamina, and all other skills necessary to perform the duties. Assume, however, that his or her English-language skills are limited. An easy accommodation would be to have the employee participate in language training. In the meantime, a notice could be prepared and the cab driver would hand it to each customer. The notice, in English, could contain the following language:

> I have been selected because of my high level of skills to work as a cab driver for this firm. I am participating in an English-language training program to improve my English skills. So that there is no mix-up, please be so kind as to write in the space below your destination:

Mealey suggests that in other contexts, employers could use other methods such as visual observation, quality control checks, or hiring supervisors who speak the same language to monitor employees' work and assist them (p. 433). Matsuda suggests using visual backups, writing memos, using pictographs, using sign language, training employees in both speaking and listening skills, and minimizing opportunities for miscommunication by standardizing procedures as simple and cost effective accommodations regarding speech differences (p. 1380). She asks us to consider the Chinese restaurant menu that allows a customer to point to number 4 if he or she has trouble pronouncing Chinese names, or a pictograph for "children crossing" that conveys an important message without verbal or written words. The methods for accommodation of persons with limited English skills, while those persons acquire such skills, are restricted only by the creativity of the teams of management, employees, and outside consultants who address remediation. Fair minded people should have no difficulty in arriving at mutually agreeable accommodations that will prevent the much more costly and inefficient litigation resolution methods from coming into play.

Educating the entire work force regarding the accommodations and the need for them would also be important in promoting the good will necessary to maintain effective working relationships. Rather than attempting to impose blanket speak-English-only rules, which might soothe the inappropriate fears of monolinguals but create resentment among bilinguals, educational approaches should be used. Role-playing and other techniques could be employed to demonstrate to monolinguals that not every conversation in a foreign language is about them. Similarly, foreign language speakers could be sensitized through similar techniques to the concern that monolinguals will feel excluded and threatened if they perceive they are being spoken about. Volunteers might even be identified who would be willing to teach basic foreign language skills to monolinguals who have some interest in learning. To determine under which circumstances it is appropriate to require the use of English and only English on the job (or any other language for that matter), a careful, objective audit of the needs of the business should be conducted. A further examination should be conducted to determine whether there is any less restrictive method of meeting the needs. The EEOC Guidelines in this regard provide a good starting point. Employees facing the adoption of what they perceive to be an overly restrictive language policy should be allowed to participate in the evaluation process. As this writer suggested in 1986, an explanation by those employees, in a nonthreatening fashion, of the beauty of the language and the importance of its use to the worker might go a long way toward alleviating some of the employer's or co-workers' misgivings.

When an employer determines that the use of bilingual skills is necessary to satisfy legitimate consumer needs, the best method to avoid disputes is to identify, in advance, with the employee the particular skills needed and then compensate that employee for the use of the skill. In emergency situations, employees should be flexible enough to provide the translation, even if it was not agreed to in advance, to protect the immediate property and business interests of the employer. The opportunity for the use of bilingual skills should be made available to all workers, and not just those of one particular national origin group. Employers also should be sensitive to the *Perez* concerns that bilingual employees who use their skills are not, as a result of such efforts, denied credit for the work or restricted in access to promotions and fair evaluations.

Unions can continue to employ translators and should encourage their leaders to obtain at least some minimal proficiency in the languages of the workers. Unions can participate in assisting with the creation of language training programs.

These are but a few of the many approaches that can be taken in accommodating the business needs of the employer and the linguistic rights and concerns of the employee. Human nature being what it is, however, there may still be situations in which problems cannot be resolved prospectively. Even in those cases, alternatives exist to avoid the cost and ill will incurred in litigation.

Dispute Resolution Techniques

The first technique employed to resolve language disputes should obviously be simple communication among the parties affected. Representatives or translators could assist if for whatever reason the primary disputants were unable to communicate the concerns effectively by themselves.

If the parties cannot resolve the problem alone, or with the help of representatives, third parties might be asked to assist. The least intrusive form of third party involvement in resolving disputes is mediation. The mediator, in contrast to a judge or arbitrator, has no power to impose an outcome on disputing parties. Rather, the function of the mediator is to assist parties to reach their own agreement (Goldberg, p. 91). Professor Fuller describes the central quality of mediation as being "its capacity to reorient the parties towards each other, not by imposing rules on them, but by helping them to achieve a new and shared perception of their relationship, a perception that will redirect their attitude and dispositions toward one another" (Riskin and Westbrook, p. 95). The reader can get a more complete exposure to the processes involved in mediation by consulting materials in the bibliography. Suffice it to say at this point, the intervention by a neutral third party could greatly assist employers and employees in addressing language issues. When the parties themselve, have lost the ability, for whatever reason, to communicate with each other regarding a speak-English-only rule, a mediator might serve as a catalyst and lend a constructive posture to the discussions rather than cause further misunderstanding and polarization. An experienced mediator serves as an educator. According to Professor Fuller, the mediator can also convey each party's proposals in language that is both faithful to the desired objectives of the party and formulate it to ensure the highest degree of receptivity by the listener. One can foresee situations in the discussions of language-on-the-job issues where an effective mediator would be able to bring all parties together and alleviate unnecessary concerns while helping the parties achieve an agreement with which they could all live. There are even resources available to help identify skilled mediators. The American Arbitration Association (AAA), with headquarters at 140 West 51st Street in New York, administers a mediation program. Mediators who serve on the AAA's panel are experts in successful negotiation. They receive a fee from the parties for their services, and they are also rewarded by knowing their efforts will result in amicable settlements of disputes that would have cost substantial time and money had it been litigated.

Another alternative to litigation involving third parties is arbitration. As Murray, Rau, and Sherman note, the traditional model of arbitration is that of a private tribunal. That is, private individuals are chosen voluntarily by the parties to a dispute in preference to the "official" courts. These arbitrators are given power to hear and judge the case (p. 390). Parties can agree in advance to submit to binding arbitration under which their arbitrator's decision will have the force of law or to a nonbinding form in which the arbitrator's decision is merely advisory to the parties. Among the reasons noted by Murray et al. for choosing arbitration rather than adjudication in dispute resolution is the speed available. Litigation may take years; arbitration can be conducted as soon as the parties agree on an arbitrator and the rules of their proceeding. Arbitration proceedings are relatively informal. An arbitration hearing, unlike a trial, is not open to the public, and unless the result of the proceeding becomes subject to court litigation, it is not a matter of public record. Also, the parties themselves are able to choose their own arbitrators. Even if they cannot agree on a total panel of arbitrators, other mechanisms can be employed, such as one side choosing one arbitrator, the other side choosing another, and then both of those arbitrators choosing the third member of a panel. The American Arbitration Association affords experienced arbitrators. The AAA provides, free of charge, clauses, rules and forms applicable to specific types of dispute free of charge.

Arbitration is more formal than mediation and is governed by federal and state statutes. Court decisions involving the use of arbitration in the context of Title VII cases raise some concerns regarding its application to language rights cases. Among these concerns is that the invocation of arbitration (or any other dispute resolution technique) will not stop the time limits from running under Title VII or other laws protecting against discrimination. That is, if an employee proceeds to an alternative technique and does not file a complaint of discrimination with the EEOC or with an appropriate court and the time limit for bringing the action expires, the employee would lose the right to bring the case in court. If the language rights case is brought to arbitration and is framed as a Title VII concern, it is also important to note that the U.S. Supreme Court has held that, notwithstanding a federal policy favoring arbitration in employment disputes, Title VII allows for a trial even after the arbitrator's decision is announced. In other words, even if arbitration is invoked and even if a "final" arbitration award is entered, employees could still proceed to federal court and obtain a new hearing on the Title VII claim if the time limits have been met. Thus, from the employer's perspective, arbitration may not be the last word and may not be an effective way of precluding access to courts. From the perspective of the employees, one commentator has suggested that arbitration is an appropriate vehicle for resolving employment discrimination disputes that are factual in nature and require only the application of established law. Employment discrimination cases raising unsettled issues of public law, he concludes, should be left to the courts and administrative agencies (99 Harv. L. Rev. 668 (1986)). Malin and Stallworth present a detailed analysis in a 1990 *Seton Hall Law Review* article concerning affirmative action issues in the role of external law and labor arbitration for the reader seeking more detailed exposure to these issues.

Beyond mediation and arbitration, there are any number of mixed processes that could be invoked in an attempt to resolve language rights issues. These alternatives may not be appropriate in every circumstance. The features that make them attractive to one party (speed, lack of application of precedent, private as opposed to public forum) might not always meet the needs of all parties. It is easy to conceive of a plaintiff willing to bear the cost and burden of litigation to win a principle not only for that individual employee but also one which will apply regionally or even nationwide. That type of precedent will not obtain from the alternative dispute resolution processes and, as noted, invocation of these processes will not preclude a lawsuit filed within the appropriate statutes of limitation.

Beyond Mere Economics

It should not be difficult for employers, employees, and unions to identify the inefficiency and impracticability of overly restrictive language policies. After all, it should be obvious that in an increasingly diverse population, the need for interaction with people from a wide variety of backgrounds is also going to increase. On a recent trip to New York City, this author was struck with the difficulties which would confront a person who did not want to engage in commercial transactions with someone who looked or sounded "foreign". That person would have great difficulty travelling in a cab or on a bus, and would almost certainly eventually die from starvation given the diverse backgrounds of workers in restaurants, cafes, and grocery stores.

However, in constructing models for preventing language-on-the-job problems and resolving them outside of litigation, economic efficiency alone should not be the basis for the efforts. The long and proud history of this nation in regard to the civil rights of its peoples does not rely upon a finding that we should respect human rights only where an economic benefit results. Rather, we have identified moral bases for abolishing slavery, affording women the right to vote, enacting numerous civil rights statutes, and receiving judicial recognition of the inalienable human rights that we choose to recognize and protect. That an economic benefit results from a morally sound position should be considered a positive, but incidental benefit to be gained.

In language-on-the-job issues, the ultimate resolution of these matters will occur when we recognize that it is wrong to cause economic hardship to someone because he or she sounds different to us. With this recognition, our courts and participants in the marketplace should have little difficulty in making the accommodations necessary as we once again experience the growing pains that have helped forge the United States into a multicultural nation.

Bibliography

Books

1. Stephen B. Goldberg, Eric D. Green, Frank E. A. Sander, *Dispute Resolution* (1985).

2. John S. Murray, Alan Scott Rau, Edward Sherman, *Processes of Dispute Resolution* (1989).

3. Leonard L. Riskin, James E. Westbrook, *Dispute Resolution and Lawyers, abridged ed.* (1987).

Articles

1. Harry T. Edwards, *Alternative Dispute Resolution: Panacea or Anathema?* 99 Harv. L. Rev. 668 (1986).

2. Patricia Ettrick, *College Preparatory Curriculum Proposed for New York City High Schools*, 1 Hispanic Outlook in Higher Education no. 11, p. 12 (June 1991).

3. David L. Gregory, *Union Leadership and Workers' Voices: Meeting the Needs of Linguistically Heterogeneous Union Members*, 58 Cinc. L. Rev. 115 (1989).

4. Martin H. Malin & Lamont E. Stallworth, *Affirmative Action Issues and the Role of External Law in Labor Arbitration*, 20 Seton Hall Law Review 745 (1990).

5. Mari J. Matsuda, *Voices of America: Accent, Antidiscrimination Law and a Jurisprudence for the Last Reconstruction*, 100 Yale L. J. 1329 (1991).

6. Linda M. Mealey, Note, *English-Only Rules and "Innocent" Employees: Clarifying National Origin Discrimination and Disparate Impact Theory Under Title VII*, 74 Minn. L. Rev. 387 (1989).

7. Bill Piatt, *Linguistic Diversity on the Airwaves: Spanish Language Broadcasting and the FCC*, 1 La Raza L. J. 101 (1984).

8. Bill Piatt, *Spanish on the Job: Business Needs and Employee Rights*, "La Voz del Llano," Kansas Advisory Committee on Hispanic Affairs, Vol. 5 No. 4 (July 1986).

Judicial Decision

1. *Alexander v. Gardner-Denver Co.*, 415 U.S. 36 (1974).

Other Materials

1. American Arbitration Association, *A Guide to Mediation for Busi-ness People,* AAA 165-15M-10/90.

2. American Arbitration Association, *Resolving Your Disputes, AAA* 155-10M-10/90.

Table of Cases

Index

Language on the Job was designed by Harold Augustus,
and composed on the AST 386/25, using PageMaker 4.0 software with
Times Roman from the Adobe Type Library.
It was printed and bound by BookCrafters, Inc.,
on acid-free Glatfelter paper.